The Window Shop

The Window Shop

Safe Harbor for Refugees
1939–1972

Ellen Miller
Ilse Heyman
Dorothy Dahl

iUniverse, Inc.
New York Lincoln Shanghai

The Window Shop
Safe Harbor for Refugees
1939–1972

iUniverse books may be ordered through booksellers or by contacting:

iUniverse
2021 Pine Lake Road, Suite 100
Lincoln, NE 68512
www.iuniverse.com
1-800-Authors (1-800-288-4677)

Because of the dynamic nature of the Internet, any Web addresses
or links contained in this book may have changed
since publication and may no longer be valid.

ISBN: 978-0-595-40620-3 (pbk)
ISBN: 978-0-595-84987-1 (ebk)

Printed in the United States of America

To the women and men of the Window Shop

Contents

Appendix

Illustrations

Unless otherwise indicated, all photos are reprinted by permission of the Schlesinger Library, Radcliffe Institute, Harvard University.

Margaret Earhart Smith
Linzer Torte (photo courtesy of Ellen Miller)

Cover photographs: Top, 102 Mount Auburn Street, 1940. Board Member Bessie Jones looks in the window. Mary Mohrer is visible inside.
Bottom, In the Gift Shop, circa 1940. Lore Kadden (Lindenfeld) shows Board Member Mrs. Percy Bridgman a bottle.
Back cover: Cock horse logo designed by Gyorgy Kepes. (Photo courtesy of Mark L. Lurie)

Acknowledgments

This book owes its existence to the women and men of the Window Shop who wrote, told, and in many other ways chronicled its history for future generations.

The authors are indebted to Diana Carey and the staff of the Schlesinger Library at Harvard University, for making the Window Shop archives available for research, and to its archivist, Katherine Kraft, for expertly cataloging the collection.

Our thanks go to Jack Alexander, Bob Alexander, Robert and Margaret Cope, George Perutz, Eva Schiffer, and Renate Benfey Wilkins for sharing their materials and photographs with us. Thanks to Mark L. Lurie, grandson-in-law of Alice Cope, for the photo of the Cock Horse sign on the back cover. We also thank Doris Martin, longtime head baker, who tested the recipes and invited us to sample them (to our delight!). Heather Hedden designed our Web site and produced the index, for which we thank her.

We thank those who pored over the manuscript and provided excellent suggestions: Eliza Cope Harrison, Dorothy Kaufmann, Joyce Majewski, Bob and Sally Alexander, Philip Somervell, Eva Moseley, and Shulamit Reinharz.

Special thanks are due to Paul Herzan, whose generous gift made publication of this book possible. Doctors Louis and Kathleen Mogul, Susan and Philip Schwarz, Theresa Gottfried, and Laurel Cates also supported the publication effort, for which we are most grateful.

We are indebted beyond words to Peter Kuttner of Cambridge Seven Associates, Inc., for cover, book design, and production assistance.

Ellen Miller
Ilse Heyman
Dorothy Dahl

The always artfully designed display case outside the Gift Shop.

Preface

From its beginning in 1939, the Window Shop of Cambridge, Massachusetts, provided a safe harbor for hundreds of German and Austrian refugees who fled from Hitler to America. It was founded by concerned Cambridge residents who were guided only by their desire to help the refugees, and over time it evolved into a nonprofit enterprise that was unparalleled in its success and influence.

That year, with pooled resources of $65, four wives of Harvard professors founded a small consignment shop in Harvard Square where refugee women could sell handmade crafts and Viennese pastries. They called it the Window Shop because the one small room had a large window. After a two-year struggle to survive and a move to a larger space, its Gift and Dress Shop was selling hand-crafted goods made mostly by refugees, and its Restaurant/Bakery was serving Viennese pastries never before seen in Harvard Square.

In 1941 the Window Shop incorporated; members of its board of directors were Christian and Jewish, and most were women. The staff were Jewish women, most of whom were refugees from Nazism. The women on the board were generous, compassionate, and energetic; they worked hand in hand with the refugees to build a dynamic, progressive workplace that was also a haven for the dispirited and displaced. While the women of the Window Shop predated the Feminist Movement, they embodied the strength, courage, energy, and vision of true feminists. Their remarkable partnership, built on mutual respect, hard work, and entrepreneurship, became the Window Shop's foundation and its legacy.

Eventually, the organization not only sold elegant European products and served delicious Continental meals; it also provided employment for German and Austrian women who had never worked outside the home and offered counseling to help them cope with their new lives. Their husbands had to retrain before they could find work, leaving the women to support the family (most refugee families arrived in the United States almost penniless). In addition to finding jobs, the women had to learn English, adjust to a different culture, cope with husbands who were uncomfortable with working wives, and care for their children. Window Shop volunteers helped them get a start in their new country, and a powerful bond was soon forged among the disparate members of the small community.

"We were like a family," said a former employee from Germany, now ninety-three years old. "We really had a sense of togetherness."

The Window Shop's profits, which increased slowly, were earmarked for the Assistance Fund, established in 1943 to help employees and their families with child care, summer camp, tuition, and emergency relief. This later became a Scholarship Fund that assisted students in the wider Cambridge community.

From 1939 to 1972 the Window Shop occupied a special place in the often turbulent lives of the immigrants it served. Because of the shop, many achieved success in their new world. Generations of Cambridge residents and Harvard and Massachusetts Institute of Technology faculty and students shopped there, worked there, volunteered there, and met there for coffee and pastries. Eleanor Roosevelt came for lunch on several occasions, bought gifts for family members at the Gift Shop, and wrote about it in her newspaper column.

But the glory days ended in 1972, partly because of sweeping changes in the commercial culture of Harvard Square, which sent sales in both the Gift Shop and the Restaurant plummeting. The Window Shop closed, but until 1987 its Scholarship Fund continued to help a new generation of immigrants, mostly students at Boston-area colleges who came from many different countries.

It was fortuitous that in the mid-eighties, Board President Dorothy Dahl recognized the value of documenting the Window Shop story to allow future historians to study not only its response to a historic catastrophe, but also how it adapted to changing circumstances, keeping the aim of the institution squarely on helping deserving people. Under Mrs. Dahl's leadership, many employees, customers, and board members were interviewed and also asked to rummage in their files and attics for minutes of meetings, letters, notes, photographs, recipes, and anecdotes. The recipes in particular proved difficult to document, since the amounts of the ingredients were gargantuan, suitable for baking upward of eight cakes at a time, and all knowledgeable cooks and bakers asked for time to experiment to reduce the recipes to a more acceptable size, like six or eight portions.

Finding a home for this material was easy—the Arthur and Elizabeth Schlesinger Library on the History of Women in America, then part of Harvard University's Radcliffe College, was a close neighbor of the Window Shop. More important, it was then and remains today the foremost library of women's history in the country. Mrs. Dahl worked with Katherine Kraft, Schlesinger Library archivist, to catalog the shop's files. A contribution from the disbanded Scholarship Fund to the Schlesinger Library defrayed the cost of processing and maintaining the collection, which is available to the public. A summary of the Window Shop records at the Schlesinger Library, prepared by archivist Eva Moseley, appears in the Appendix.

Utilizing this valuable collection, *The Window Shop* tells the complete history of the organization. The themes developed in this work are multifaceted. The heart of the book reveals a unique vision and partnership among a small group of Harvard wives and a growing number of Jewish refugee women. The collaboration and mutual respect that grew between two such disparate communities provide valuable research material in cross-cultural studies, the historic upheavals of the 1930s and 1940s, and the entrepreneurial spirit.

Furthermore, research into the refugee women's lives reveals the divisive sociological dilemmas they faced in suddenly having become their families' sole support when their husbands could not find work in their professions. For the wife of a German or Austrian doctor or lawyer, the social stigma of being a waitress or a bus girl in the Window Shop restaurant was, at first, difficult to overcome. "If someone would have told me in Germany I would be selling pastries or waiting on tables," said an employee, "I would have said, 'You are nuts!' But we needed the money, and it didn't bother me."

In all cases, Window Shop board members tried to help by finding jobs for the newcomers within the organization, in addition to providing counseling, referrals, English lessons, and financial assistance for child care and tuition. Coworkers, who were also refugees, offered friendship, support, and shared experiences.

The Window Shop story is told by the women who were responsible for its surprising success—the refugees, the Harvard wives, the customers, the board members. Their own words have been preserved in oral histories, speeches, letters, documents, and other records at the Schlesinger Library. A small number of Window Shop employees and board members are still living; their oral histories were recently recorded for this book, and several family members also contributed their reminiscences. We have attempted to present the history of the Window Shop as accurately and completely as possible, with the aim of capturing the spirit and essence of this remarkable place.

The book is organized chronologically as well as by subject matter. Each chapter begins with a brief overview of the period, followed by the "voices" of those who participated in it. A biographical section called "Portraits" begins on page 97.

The reader may notice that we refer to some members of the Window Shop by their first names and others by their surnames; this practice reflects the times and various cultures of the Window Shop.

Chronology of Events

1939   May 2: Window Shop opens at 37 Church Street with Mary Mohrer first employee.

November: Moves to 102 Mount Auburn Street, opens Tea Room and Pastry Shop.

1940   Jan. 8: Opens Restaurant to serve lunch.

1941   March 13: Incorporates as charitable organization, with Margaret Earhart Smith as first president (1941–42).

April, May: Appoints first executive committee, changes its composition.

Summer: Remodels 102 Mount Auburn.

1942   Jan. 24: Friendship House opens in lunchroom in evenings.

January: Begins serving dinners.

March 9: Establishes Committee on Personnel Practices.

Fall: Elsa Ulich becomes president (1942–48).

Appoints Mary Mohrer manager of Gift Shop, Alice Broch manager of kitchen.

1943   Scholarship Fund established with Koch linens.

Provides accident and sickness insurance.

Spring: Closes Friendship House.

1946   Purchases Cock Horse Inn on Brattle Street.

1947   Opens on Brattle Street in March after remodeling.

1948   Renames Assistance Fund after Elsa Ulich.

Alice Cope elected president (1948–54).

1949   June 11: Celebrates tenth anniversary with fashion show.

1950   April: Purchases and renovates adjoining 5 Story Street property.

1954   Elects Elizabeth Aub president (1954–64).

1958   Implements employee life insurance plan.

1964   May: Elects Dorothy Dahl president (1964–68).
        Alice Broch retires.

1968   Elects Marion Bever president (1968–72).

1971   October: Closes Restaurant, reopens as Viennese café with limited menu.

1972   Closes Gift Shop and café.
        Sells property to Cambridge Center for Adult Education.
        Elects Richard Kahan president (1972–74).

1971   Elects Anne Harken president (1974–79).

1978   August: Consents to demolition by Cambridge Center of former premises except Blacksmith House.

1979   Again elects Dorothy Dahl president (1979–87).

1987   April: Dissolves, leaving money to longtime employees on the retirement plan and to Radcliffe College, Northeastern University, and The Boston Foundation.

Window Shop Bakery and Tea Room staff (in the snow!) at 102 Mount Auburn Street.

One

In the Beginning

"Only in Cambridge." A 1972 notice in the *Boston Globe* opened with these words, as the legendary Window Shop closed its doors and sold its historic house to the Cambridge Center for Adult Education. The obituary detailed its beginnings in 1939 in a room over what is now a restaurant at 37 Church Street, its move to larger quarters on Mount Auburn Street, and its final home on Brattle Street, where it became a famous Restaurant/Bakery and Gift and Dress Shop.

Only in Cambridge? Perhaps, because other, similar organizations had opened in other cities, but they lacked the Window Shop's success and longevity.[1] Cambridge in the 1930s was the fourth-largest manufacturing town in the Commonwealth of Massachusetts, well-known for its innovations and inventions. Within its boundaries were four major colleges: Harvard University and Radcliffe College in Harvard Square, Massachusetts Institute of Technology

(MIT), and Lesley College. Across the Charles River were Boston University, Boston College, Simmons College, Northeastern University, the Harvard Medical School, and an associated complex of hospitals, as well as such specialized schools as the New England Conservatory of Music, the Boston Conservatory, the Museum School of the Boston Museum of Fine Arts, and Wentworth Institute. Nearby were Tufts University and Wellesley College.

For many students, undergraduate and graduate, Harvard Square was a focal point—old movies, new music and styles, and a variety of performances both indoors and outdoors all made the Square vibrant. "Funky, eclectic, original" describes the Harvard Square of the period, according to a longtime resident.

The Cambridge environment and the active refugee support network in the area attracted Jewish German and Austrian refugees, whose cultural and intellectual interests were compatible with those of the residents who welcomed them. In addition, it was an attractive environment for women.

"Brilliant women in academia and in the professions have found Cambridge a hospitable place to live," wrote Marion Cannon Schlesinger.[2] "It is interesting that distinguished women psychoanalysts like Helene Deutsch and Grete Bibring found a haven in Cambridge after their flight from Hitler ... and that they were instrumental in making Cambridge and Boston one of the most significant centers for psychoanalysis in the western hemisphere."[3]

Much of the Cambridge academic and professional community had close personal ties to Europe through family, friends, professional, or business contacts. The shock of learning, sometimes firsthand, how the Nazi takeover starting in 1933 was affecting German colleagues galvanized these residents to "do something." Working with area refugee organizations, they helped Jewish refugees become acclimated to their new lives through counseling and by finding jobs, housing, and child care for them. The Window Shop soon became the focus for this critical activity.

Refugees from Hitler's Europe who came to Cambridge found an established, thriving, and welcoming Jewish community, estimated at ten thousand people, whose roots reached back to the mid-nineteenth century. There were four active synagogues in Cambridge and a number of kosher butchers. But inevitably, incidents of anti-Semitism were as common here as elsewhere in the country: "Anti-Semitic gangs beat up the Jewish valedictorian of Cambridge High and Latin in our class," recalls a longtime Jewish resident of Cambridge.[4]

In the heart of Cambridge, Harvard University's "genteel anti-Semitism" before and just after World War II was reflected in its notorious quota system and its friendliness toward Nazi-controlled universities.[5] Although Harvard President James Bryant Conant's anti-Semitic remarks were limited to his private correspondence, Morton Keller, coauthor of *Making Harvard Modern*,[6] was quoted in the *Boston Globe* of November 21, 2005: "Conant ... was pretty bad initially at reacting to the Nazis," but as the 1930s progressed, "he had a strong desire to see the best students and the best faculty come to Harvard, and I think that outweighed his anti-Semitism."

Professor Alan Dershowitz of Harvard Law School described the university of the 1930s: "Prior to World War II the number of Jewish professors at Harvard Law School could be counted on one hand. And the law school was considered progressive on these matters. The university itself, particularly the college, was worse. In all of its history, there had never been a Jewish dean at Harvard.... Harvard's history of discrimination against Jews is fairly typical of that of other major universities. Indeed, it reflects the condition of Jews in elite American institutions and professions during the first half of this century."[7]

There was more anti-Semitism during the war than at any other time in American history. Once the war began, only 21,000 persons from Germany and Austria were admitted, 10 percent of the number allowed under the 1924 McCarran-Walter quota law, a reaction to public hostility across the country. Patriotic groups like the Veterans of Foreign Wars and the American Legion called for a total ban on immigration.[8] Almost 190,000 quota places were deliberately left unused.

Following the war, in 1948, Congress passed the Displaced Persons Act, authorizing two hundred thousand Displaced Persons to enter the United States. The act was amended in 1950 to make it more favorable to Jewish Displaced Persons. The law expired in 1952, by which time more than eighty thousand Jews had immigrated to the United States with the aid of Jewish agencies. Included in this wave of immigration were German-Jewish scientists, technicians, and professionals.

The refugees who came to the Boston area found diverse organizations dedicated to helping them, and many volunteers turned their talents to the new Window Shop. The Christian Committee for Refugees and its executive director, Norman Goehring, worked closely with local churches. It sponsored and ran Goodwill Houses in Groton and Marshfield, Massachusetts, and a Refugee Guest House at 17 Francis Avenue in Cambridge. Its board of directors included many Harvard professors—Kirtley Mather, Paul Sachs, Donald Scott, and Percy Bridgman among them. This organization was the source of exceptional volunteers—Margaret Smith, Alice Cope, and Elsa Ulich all became leaders in the Window Shop enterprise. The Window Shop Restaurant was enriched by refugees such as Lotte Benfey, who came from a responsible position in the Groton Goodwill House.

The Boston Committee for Refugees, directed by Benjamin Selekman, was a remarkable organization. It was affiliated with Jewish Philanthropies, sometimes referred to as the Jewish Committee and, after 1935, the Boston Committee. This volunteer organization included the Hebrew Immigrant Aid Society (HIAS), which met boats carrying refugees, helped them settle, and were tireless in their efforts. A Mr. Jacobs who worked there was referred to by Window Shop Board Member Bessie Jones as "a saintly character," who steered her to the Window Shop as a volunteer. He also was important in introducing Mary Mohrer, a young Viennese refugee, to one of the founders of the Window Shop. She became its first employee and thirty-three years later closed its doors for the last time.

There were government agencies and individuals—the U.S. Commission for Refugees; the Massachusetts Displaced Persons Commission; and a remarkable woman, Alice W. O'Connor, a supervisor of Social Services in the Commonwealth's Division of Immigration and Americanization, who gave dedicated and thoughtful service to refugees. The private sector had many refugee-related organizations, including the American Friends Service Committee, the Boston Provident Society, the Physicians' Committee for Refugees, a Lawyers' Committee, and Youth Aliyah of the Women's Division of Jewish Philanthropies. All of these organizations were supportive at some time of Window Shop employees.

In addition to the relief organizations, many individuals found ways to help the refugees and to promote tolerance and understanding in the community. Paul Sachs of the Fogg Art Museum was effective in helping refugee art historians, and Percy W. Bridgman closed his noted Harvard astronomy laboratories to visitors from totalitarian countries, prompting the *Harvard Crimson*, the student newspaper, to comment that this was "one of the most outspoken denunciations of the Fascist states yet made by anyone in high Faculty circles."[9] Professor Robert Ulich of the Harvard School of Education, the husband of Elsa Brändström Ulich, headed a committee to sponsor refugee scholars in early 1939. Twenty-five were selected to come to the United States and were financed.[10]

Famed astronomer Dr. Harlow Shapley of the Harvard Smithsonian Astrophysical Observatory was largely responsible for the Asylum Fellowship Plan at Harvard, a two-year plan under which the university added sixteen academic refugees from Europe to its permanent staff. Sixteen others were given emergency appointments, a necessary prelude to enable these men to avoid the concentration camps of Europe.[11]

In 1939 a group of MIT and Harvard professors organized a boycott of German-manufactured scientific supplies to "protest against Nazi attitudes toward Science and Scientists." Books, considered to be the result of individual work, were excluded from the boycott.

"One cannot take history for granted," said Professor Howard Mumford Jones, husband of Bessie Jones, in 1938 as he organized an optional course at Harvard in American history. Other professors added courses—for example, Carl J. Friedrich on Propaganda and Public Opinion, Seymour Harris on Economic Aspects of War, and Gordon Allport on Psychological Phases of Propaganda.

Harvard students were active in organizations like the World Student Service Fund, the Phillips Brooks House, and other international student relief organizations. At Lowell House in 1938 students drew up a plan "to open Harvard to refugees," whereby Harvard would provide tuition, and the students would pay for room and board. The Harvard Corporation voted funds for scholarships for "Nazi Refugees Regardless of Creed," and all over Cambridge public forums were held and speeches were given.[12]

For refugees newly arrived from the horrors of Hitler's Europe, the Window Shop was indeed a haven. The taint of anti-Semitism did not enter its doors, and the compassionate, welcoming people within—the board members and staff—offered a lifeline to the newcomers. Before the Window Shop board members and staff could help, however, they had to understand the condition of the new immigrants.

Contemporary author Jhumpa Lahiri, whose parents are Indian, writes often of "the loneliness of dislocation" that afflicts all immigrants, and countless works of fiction and movies eloquently describe the plight of those exiled from their homeland.[13] Not only had the wartime and postwar refugees experienced the most serious dislocation, often having moved several times before reaching these shores, but many had suffered the brutality of the concentration camps. Some were the sole survivors of their families. Physical and psychological wounds were profound and long lasting. Many families were forced to deal with a dynamic radically different from the familiar European tradition in which the father is the breadwinner and the mother is a housewife. Now the men, often from the professional class in Germany and Austria, had to be retrained to work in the United States. How does one "retrain" if one's earlier job title had been Chief Justice of Economic Arbitration in the Weimar Republic? The women, most of whom had never worked outside the home, became the breadwinners, rolling up their sleeves and working as cleaning women, housekeepers, and governesses. Family tension, if not outright dysfunction, became part of the refugee experience.

With emotional and financial support, the Window Shop refugees eventually found their way toward becoming productive citizens and were proud to be called "New Americans" in recognition of the expectation that they would become U.S. citizens.

At the Window Shop's twentieth anniversary, Board Member Marion Muller summarized the importance of Cambridge to the Window Shop's success:

> From the beginning Cambridge people have supported the Window Shop. When the Shop began to make profits and needed to set up a bookkeeping system, MIT loaned two men from their Business Administration Department to do the job. One of them became interested enough to serve as treasurer until he was called by the Navy. The

Cambridge Trust Company in the person of Mr. George Macomber has been our friend and financed our moving and building projects. Many friends have tided us over financial crises. And thousands of people have been good customers and spoken kind words. Perhaps the general attitude of Cambridge toward the Shop has been the most important support. The Shop, with its European atmosphere, food, clothes, gifts, and foreign accents, has been cordially accepted. Similar enterprises have started in other communities. None, I am told, have survived for twenty years. So the Window Shop has become a Cambridge institution.

Voices

"Toward the middle of April 1933, we both realized that it was impossible for us to stay in Berlin [where my husband was working with a German colleague]. Having seen a man being dragged through the street by his hair and hearing each day of someone's laboratory or library being destroyed, we decided we could not stay in Germany. I, twenty-four years old, never touched by man's cruelty, terrified by what we saw in the streets every day, was a burden to my husband. We decided to go to London which, in the original plan, was to have been for a few months at the end of our stay in Europe.

"To this day, I can feel the relief of safely crossing the border into Holland. We were carrying letters from the Austrian Consul and from other friends. I was wearing jewelry that certainly was not mine. We were happy that we could help the refugees who often were only passing through London on their way to the United States or Canada.

"That is, very briefly, how my husband and I began to be a part of the network which cared for the Hitler Refugees....

"The New England Christian Committee for Refugees was helping to settle some of the refugees. Perhaps I should explain for a minute why the word Christian was in the committee's name. It offended many people, and some new Americans would not go to the committee for help. However, the founders of the committee and the volunteers who worked for it had good reason for including the word 'Christian.' They realized that churches and their parishioners were seeing the Hitler disaster as a Jewish problem. Some way had to be found not only to help the already overburdened Jewish community, but to open the eyes and hearts of so-called Christians in New England. Thus the committee was born. It was helpful in finding homes, jobs, and English lessons for the newcomers. It opened doors which never would have been opened without their volunteers' persistence.

"The committee supported the idea of the Window Shop from the very beginning, both financially and with volunteers."

Alice Cope

"What I did a couple of times was to go down and meet the boats. One of our board members was very active in the Hebrew Immigrant Aid Society—HIAS. He used to ask for volunteers. Here were these mostly families, absolutely bewildered, scared to death. And what you did was, you had papers to hand them, to tell them where to go. I could speak German which was a help; not terrific German, but it was very useful because I could understand them. I would tell them where to find out about housing, where to find things, etc."

Marion Bever

"The greatest boost came when the Rev. Endicott Peabody, headmaster of the Groton School, offered a job to one of our most able and distinguished [refugees]. By this action of Rev. Peabody and the extraordinary personalities of the man and his wife whom Rev. Peabody chose, many of the obstacles for refugee teachers were overcome. Many years later, I was told by a graduate of Groton how much he had learned from this refugee couple and from Rev. Peabody's 'Christian act.' All this led to the Window Shop."

Alice Cope

"We have felt that what the newcomer needed more than anything else was a sense of belonging, a feeling of the team, a place where human profits are more important than money profits, a place where the newcomer could gradually forget the horrors of concentration camps, and a place where different languages, cultures, and backgrounds could meet. Over the years we have had German, Austrian, Czech, Polish, Hungarian, Romanian, English, French, Italian, Yugoslav, Greek, Chinese, Japanese, Russian, Latvian, Norwegian, Swedish, Israeli, Syrian, and Indian newcomers pass through our Shop."

Anonymous board member

"[Lotte Benfey] never stopped talking thankfully about the chance the Window Shop gave her husband to work. He was Chief Justice of the Supreme Court of Economic Arbitration in the Weimar Republic. It was a little difficult to place him. We did; he worked for nine years [copying menus, among other tasks] and made them both happy."

Letter from Alice Broch to Dorothy Dahl, July 9, 1987

"Sometimes those [refugees] who had finally reached a haven after so many stops on the way were simply too exhausted to face the new situation. They needed to be cared for and looked after for a while. Elsa Brändström sought places where they could recuperate in boardinghouses or in the country homes of friends. During this period she received magnanimous offers....

"In 1937, after [the Ulichs'] return from a trip to Europe, Elsa Brändström collected furniture and home equipment for the refugees, because the later the refugees came the less they had. In addition to educators and businessmen, artists and technically trained persons, the immigrant lists now included more and more workers, domestic employees and craftsmen. To help these people was particularly difficult: torn from a fixed and stable circle of community life, without language skills, knowing only the people of their village, street or town, America must have seemed to them an enormous giant."

"Das Leben der Elsa Brändström" by Magdalena Padberg

"In Vienna, given the elevated station to which [my father's] professional status had accustomed him, it would have been unthinkable for my mother, who had a background in business management, to be anything but his lady of the house. He was the typical Central European husband who was, and was determined to remain, incapable of boiling an egg or finding, let alone choosing, his own underwear or tie. My mother, who was passionately devoted to fulfilling his every wish, was certainly content to wait on him, hand and foot. Prevailing upon him, once they left Vienna, to let her complement, at times take over, his breadwinning function did not, I am quite sure, represent a sacrifice of pride for her as it probably did for him."

Eva Schiffer

"The war had begun. Many Window Shop employees knew of close relatives and friends in Germany who could not escape.... In addition, America too had begun its war preparations and had increased its propaganda against the aggressors. Voices were beginning to be heard, asking whether evicted former German citizens were not still Germans. There was even talk of Nazi infiltration through the refugees. The reciprocal distrust grew. After the Japanese attack on Pearl Harbor ... the official designation for former citizens of the axis powers was to be 'enemy aliens.'

"Elsa Brändström gave a talk about the situation of the refugees, pleading with her American friends to understand the inner conflict of people who once had civil rights in Central Europe and had not yet become established overseas. Soon after, she was asked to become president of the Window Shop."

"Das Leben der Elsa Brändström" by Magdalena Padberg

"There was a family—the woman had never had a job, the man was a physician. She knew how to sew, and she did some sewing for us. They had a child.... In Europe, this man (I'll call him Dr. B.) had been a rather prominent physician. Here, he had to work under another man. His ego was so badly hurt that he suffered terribly. The hospital he worked in was an anti-alcoholic center. The wife would call me in the middle of the night and say that he was near a nervous breakdown and would I come.... I would go over there, and I would just sit and listen to him and tell him this was a new country, that he had this job and it was in the medical field, and that things would change once he had passed his exams again.

"One day she came with a package. I opened it, and there was a dress she had made for me. How she could make a dress without my trying it on at all was unbelievable. I'm still, when I think of it today, deeply, deeply touched, because she had a household, a small child, she worked for a living, and she had a husband who was near a nervous breakdown."

Mary Mohrer

"My father had his hands full with improving his English and competing with students more than twenty years younger than he, as he worked his way into an unfamiliar approach to the practice of law.... Moreover, clearly America was a country of wonders. My father was convinced of it one day when we had a problem with some pipes, and the plumber arrived in his own car!"

Eva Schiffer

"It is only now that I fully appreciate the challenges they faced. For my father, it meant loss of profession, since his training as a lawyer was not transferable, and he was certainly too old to begin again. He went to night school to study accounting while working as a bookkeeper/clerk during the day. Yet after four years of this, his vision had so deteriorated that he had to give up his plan to become an accountant.

"My mother began to give piano lessons, which was a transferable skill, yet English, which for her was a fourth language, presented a formidable challenge. After a Christmas job at Goren's in Central Square selling toys, the Window Shop offered me a job as a bus girl two evenings a week and on weekends."

Nadia Ehrlich Finkelstein

"One of the agencies was most unfriendly and told me that they did not have any jobs for foreigners. And then I looked up some of the advertisements from the papers. Some of them were very dismal looking places, but I thought it would be interesting to see what people had to say. One was more unpleasant than anybody I have met in a long time. He said that the Jews and the Germans had started that war, that they were spread everywhere to poison people's opinion, that everywhere they were trying to get influence and to govern the world."

Letter from Annegrete Levens to Margaret Smith

"At the Window Shop were people whose husbands had very high positions in Europe. If the husband had a title in Vienna—you carried your title whether you were a physician or a lawyer or a chemist, a physicist—anybody who had a Ph.D. was called *Doktor*. Not only he but his wife received the *Doktor* as well. She was *Frau Doktor,* and she immediately belonged to a higher sphere really. When they came to this country, some of them sold behind the counter at the Window Shop, some worked in the kitchen.

"Boston had an Austrian Club. What struck me as so amazing was that when you came through the door of the club, the world changed. In that circle the *Frau Doktor* was again *Frau Doktor,* and she had regained her status. But she didn't suffer having lost it. But of course the Window Shop was protected employment. I don't know how these people would have felt if they'd had to work in a regular bakery. The Window Shop was not that kind of thing. That's something it should be very proud of. It did give people the feeling of dignity, no matter what they were doing. You could scrub the floors at the Window Shop. The Americans who volunteered, the president of the Shop, would all do the same. That made it even easier. It was status-free."

Mary Mohrer

"My grandmother [Hertha Becher, Bakery cashier] loved working with people and she loved working at the Window Shop. Now, looking back on it, I think she appreciated very much that she had some way to bring in some money and either take care of her own needs or contribute to the family. It gave her the feeling of self-respect, that she wasn't just the grandmother stuck off in a room someplace. She was an independent, hard-working person, so that wouldn't have agreed with her at all."

Robert Alexander

"Ours was really jobs plus. And jobs were very important, and a sense of belonging, and a sense of status. That was the big thing we offered them. They were all ladies and gentlemen working at the Window Shop. We just treated them like that. I think in the beginning they were kind of surprised that we were willing to do menial work."

Marion Bever

Mrs. Geiringer at her sewing machine.

The Gift and Dress Shop

When immigrants from Germany, Austria, and other European countries came to the United States in large numbers in the late 1930s, "they needed housing and jobs, they lacked language competency, and many were depressed and bewildered," recalled one Window Shop employee. "Men had been thrown out of good positions, academic careers, etc. Women were mostly housewives who had never held a job."

The professional men—doctors, lawyers, accountants—had to retrain before they could practice their professions here. Their wives had to support their families while husbands tried to find their way back into their professions, if they could. For most women, the overriding goal was to find employment, but English was a problem, and child care was a concern. Some women who could find neither jobs nor child care sold their handicrafts or baked Viennese pastries at home. "Mother made *Oblaten* [a thin cookie] in our kitchen in Cambridge," said the son of a Window Shop baker, "and then sold them to friends."

In 1939, encouraged by the New England Christian Committee for Refugees, four wives of Harvard professors—Mrs. James McLaughlin, Mrs. Griffin, Mrs. Willard van Orman Quine, and Mrs. Carpenter[14]—pooled a total of $65 to start a small shop where refugees could sell their homemade goods. They found afford-able space at 37 Church Street. The one small room was bare. It had an enormous window, so they called the enterprise the Window Shop. Opening day was May 2, 1939, and before the month was over, Mrs. Quine loaned another $50 to the shop to keep it going.

It is reported that Mrs. Quine herself made hats, flowers, and scarves to sell at the shop, along with some refugee sewing and secondhand items from Cantabrigians. "Hand-knitted sweaters, handmade gloves, belts, flowers, *Apfel Strudel,* and other pastries were all brought together in this little room for sale," another Window Shop staff member recalled.

That this was a shoestring operation is an understatement. Early account books list such sales as "Dainty Dot Stockings, $3.31; Handkerchiefs, $3.95; Jewelry, $7.78."[15] It surely didn't help that the founding ladies considered the Window Shop cash box their personal property: "These ladies, finding them-selves short of cash while shopping, would dash to the Window Shop and take money from the cash box (after all, it was their money!), with no idea what chaos they produced in the bookkeeping."[16]

The original founders were soon overwhelmed by the complexities of running a shop and trying to help desperate refugees. They left the Window Shop, but other energetic, capable, and strong women took their place and guided the shop in its early struggles. The first Window Shop Board of Directors consisted of five women and three men, who became the incorporators in March 1941.[17] Thereafter, they voted to increase board membership to nineteen. An executive committee was selected to manage the business.

So the Window Shop began—a small shop that evolved over a thirty-three-year period into a nonprofit Gift and Dress Shop, Restaurant and Bakery, and de facto social services agency. It became a remarkably vibrant and supportive com-munity, one that none of the founders could have imagined.

Voices

"The women who founded the Window Shop had no experience, no money, and no real idea where they were going. However, they had two good ideas, which were the background for everything that developed. One was to introduce as many as possible of the refugees in the area to Cambridge [and] to find them jobs, develop whatever talents they had, and to teach English....

"There were many groups in Boston interested in the refugees,[18] but all of them, with the exception of the Jewish groups, were amateurs and frequently were more warm-hearted than practical, more interested in telling the refugee what he should do than in helping him to find his own way in his own time. The group of Harvard wives of which I have spoken found a middle road."

Alice Cope

"My involvement with refugee problems began earlier [than 1939]. I went to Felix Frankfurter when a great many of the atrocities about Germany were coming through and said I would like to do something for refugees. Professor Frankfurter sent me to Ben Selekman, who was head of the Jewish Philanthropies organization and was also a professor at Harvard Business School. He sent me to the Boston Refugee Committee, which was being run by a man named Jacobs, a very saintly character, who looked after all the refugees that kept pouring into that office."

Bessie Jones

"One of the things I did in the Boston Jewish Committee office was to look at incoming letters from people from Germany and other European countries where these people were jeopardized, asking if there were any possibility that a member of the family of their same name lived in Boston. If so, would they be willing to supply affidavits.... One day Mr. Jacobs brought a young woman here who had just come from New York. She was a Viennese who had been doing translations for the Council of Jewish Women in New York. She did not want to stay in New York and chose to come to Boston. This was Mary Mohrer.

"I can remember exactly what she looked like that day, and one of the problems was that she had a remote relative who lived in Boston that Mr. Jacobs thought she ought to contact....

"I called up this person and said that there was a young woman here named Mary Mohrer, originally a teacher from Vienna, who was supposed to be related to him, and the committee thought he ought to know about it and to get acquainted with her. He said, 'What does she want?' I said, 'She doesn't want anything. It's just a question of getting acquainted and possibly some connection that might help.' Well, where would they meet? We lived on Memorial Drive at the time, but we had an engagement for dinner that night. I said I would give her the keys to my apartment, and she could meet him there. This was astonishing to Mary, who never supposed anybody could let a stranger into her apartment. As a matter of fact, it didn't happen, and I did not see her again until one day in the *Christian Science Monitor* I saw a photograph of her dressed in a dirndl."

Bessie Jones

"Mr. Jacobs said, 'There is a group of Cambridge women. They are all non-Jewish. They have never been interested in this problem, but somehow they suddenly became gripped by the events in Europe.' A Mrs. Quine had approached him and said that she would like very much to extend hospitality to somebody. 'You are the person she picked,' he said. 'We would like you to go to Cambridge as her guest, to begin with.'

"At Mrs. Quine's house I met a group of other women whose husbands were all connected with Harvard. Their idea was to start a thrift shop and turn the money over to the Refugee Committee. And I was looking for a job. After that meeting, they started to really plan, and they rented a room at 37 Church Street. Then one day Mrs. Quine called up and said, 'We are talking to people, and we need somebody to interpret. Can you help?' I said, 'Well, when I'm not looking for a job, I'll be glad to.'

"So on and off I interpreted Italian and French and German. And I met more people. It suddenly occurred to me that all these people, although they had never worked, knew how to do something. I suggested to Mrs. Quine, 'If you will find out what these people can do, we can just start to sell what they produce; maybe there would be more dignity in it, and the people would get the money directly. Why don't we try it?' It was early spring, 1939....

"People came. A woman made little umbrellas, and I had to write in every umbrella because it was our consignment. The amount of work with all of this was unbelievable, for 35 cents! And then a woman came and said that she could bake, so we sold cakes for 10 cents apiece. If somebody wanted to have collars or cuffs turned on a man's shirt, we found someone who could do that.

"It was a nonstop thing, because it started not to just be a buying, selling, producing thing, but it started really to be a social agency. People came with their personal problems, housing problems, psychological problems, or husbands who had big positions and finally got a position here, but their ego was so badly damaged that living with them was practically impossible. That could happen at midnight. You could get a phone call, and you would walk over and sit with them and talk with them."

Mary Mohrer

"Names and vocations of [some] of the refugees who were provided with work through the Shop

- Mrs. Brandt, wife of a temporarily unemployed accountant, sold German and Viennese candy made by refugees

- Mrs. Birnbaum, wife of a former storekeeper, employed as dressmaker

- Mrs. Van der Walde, wife of former lawyer, made artificial flowers

- Mrs. Elsberg, wife of German physician, sold homemade European perfumes

- The Misses Barsis from Vienna, knitted doilies and received many orders

- Mr. Hirsch sold film supplies

- Mrs. Jarecki invented new style of aprons

- Mr. Gottschalk, employed as carpenter

- Mrs. Schuetz, widow, provided with cleaning jobs in and through Shop

- Mr. Hansen, artist, painter, designed initials."

Report by Mary Mohrer and Herta Epstein of the
Committee for Christian Refugees

"There was one day when we didn't have the rent money. I went to the [Harvard] law school, and Professor McLaughlin loaned me $35. That was the rent. Later, when I returned it, he was very upset about it because he thought it was not a loan but a gift. I said, 'You never said it was a gift. I believe we should be self-supporting, and if we have debts, we pay them. We now have the money, and here it is.'

"One day was a turning point for the Window Shop, and it was still on Church Street. It had been hot, and I wore an Austrian dirndl. I hadn't planned to wear that, but I just couldn't iron. (At that time we ironed everything!) As I walked down the street, I had these incredible looks of people. Everybody smiled. You know, a dirndl, when you have a good figure and you are relatively young, is a very flattering gown. And it was a very original thing. The skirt was different, and the white blouse … it was really very lovely. I entered the cafeteria, and I got these compliments from everybody, even the busboy. I came to the Shop, and the *Christian Science Monitor* came. Whether it was by chance or whatever, they photographed me. The picture was in the *Monitor*, and there was a short story of the Shop. A few days later the door opened and there stood Mrs. Howard Mumford Jones—Bessie Jones. She said, 'I'm so glad I found you again!'"

Mary Mohrer

"When I saw this picture I went immediately around to Church Street where the Window Shop was and said, 'Why don't I know about this? I have been doing refugee work, and I did not know this place existed.' I was going to the country for the summer (we had a house in Peacham, Vermont), but I told Mary, 'If you get into trouble, I know someone who will help you. In the meantime you can send me some chocolate-coated almonds, which were being made by some people in New York. You could send some to the country. But if you need money, let me know.'"

Bessie Jones

"At the Shop, [Miss Mohrer] was the center of charmed comment. One customer ordered a dirndl like it, and within the week the original was on display. By the middle of August, four dirndls were on their way to Oregon in response to a single order. This lucky chance gave the impetus for one of the Shop's greatest successes in dressmaking and design."

Anonymous board member

"A Viennese-trained designer and dressmaker, Alice Boehm, did a beautiful job [of copying the dirndl], and thereafter she supplied the Window Shop with her creations for years to come. By the time the dirndl craze subsided, Alice Boehm was well established and dressed many a bride and many Cambridge ladies....

"I remember one of our older customers, a faculty wife, wanted a dirndl to wear at a party for international students. She was a short woman, as wide as she was tall. I measured her and later said to Mrs. Boehm, 'I had a hard time getting my arms around her with the tape measure. You'll have to just fudge the measurements, because you can't tell exactly where one part of her anatomy stops and another starts!'

"She also wanted a Tyrolean hat with a feather, much to Mary's distress. She protested to me, 'No, we can't do that. She will look like a fool, and people will question my integrity.' In came Dr. Helene Deutsch [the well-known psychoanalyst], one of our customers, and seeing Mary's distraught face, she asked what was the matter. When Mary told her about the hat, Dr. Deutsch said simply, 'At her age, she's entitled to look like a fool! Order her the hat!'"

Ilse Heyman

"Late that summer [1939] I got a letter from Mary saying they had no money to continue. Mrs. Clement Smith (Margaret Earhart Smith) owned a house in Peacham (that's how we happened to be there), and I rode around to her house. She gave me her check for $150, and I sent it down to Mary. After Mary paid the bills she had $11, and that's what the Window Shop was able to continue going on.

"In the meantime, I had a letter from Dorothy McLean, the wife of Saunders McLean of the Mathematics Department at Harvard. She knew about my retail and advertising experience. She wrote me and said that Mrs. Ulich and Mrs. Epstein of the Christian Committee for Refugees, who knew about the Window Shop, were very anxious that it continue, but it was threatened to close because the faculty wives who had started it were getting a little worried, as their husbands were, and they wanted to pull out.[19] I said when I got back, I would see them and also go to Church Street and see Mary, see what they had, and what I could do about it. That's what I did. I found they had almost nothing to sell except a few things that some refugees had brought in—there were little umbrellas made out of handkerchiefs, leather flowers, hand-knitted sweaters, and embroidered blouses."

Bessie Jones

"The most striking thing to Bessie Jones was that the refugee-made articles were not selling and never would, for one simple reason: nothing was styled to American tastes or American fashion. Thick-knit sweaters with short snug waists were attempting to compete with the current baggy cut and lighter wools of the American sweater. Beautiful blouses heavy with embroidery would have to be prohibitively priced to justify the time and labor spent in making them.

"There were many factors to be considered in giving advice. Here were women, many of them wives of distinguished men, used to the security of gracious and charming households but with no specific training or skills. They were uprooted and in a strange land. The new language was a handicap. The American maxim that all work commanded respect was hard to accept at once. Mrs. Jones understood all this when she undertook, as a volunteer, to advise and guide the Shop. Step by step in some cases, she showed each individual worker what had to be done and gradually developed standards of quality for everything that was to be sold in the Shop."

Anonymous board member

"I said to Mary that I could spend half days. 'If you have a census of the people who are here, send postcards to them with samples of what they can do, and we will see what we can sell and what we cannot.' They brought some things in. We sent postcards to a few and made appointments for each day. Some of them had been trained to do hand things of various kinds, which I did not believe would sell in this country, or at any rate would be too expensive. Some of them were very good knitters, but their styles were not right for American women, and they were too heavy for our well-heated houses. So we would say, 'You can knit well, but you will have to restyle.' And that went on, and in the course of events we managed to buy enough things to sell, so that into the fall of 1939, we were doing pretty well.

"I wrote about forty letters to faculty wives, and they came in. The two I remember most were Mrs. Paul Sachs and Mrs. Donald Scott, who was very generous and well-off, and who bought $40 worth of stuff one day. Mary's big blue eyes just opened wide—she had never sold that much to anybody. Mrs. Sachs was interested in the cooking aspect, and she brought her own German recipes from her own family."

Bessie Jones

"During the first part of September [1939], business was still very slow. Mrs. Clement Smith [Margaret Earhart Smith] of Brookline donated $150 to the Shop. This amount and part of the money given in August ($100) by the Committee for Christian Refugees made it possible to pay all debts and cover all expenses. We have sold $76 worth of merchandise. The dressmaking department, which already employs five dressmakers, is very busy and has prospects for more work."

Report by Mary Mohrer and Herta Epstein of the
Committee for Christian Refugees

"Well, about three weeks before Christmas [1939] the real estate man came and said, being very polite, 'Some Hebrews have bought this office building, and you will have to move.'

"I knew about 102 Mount Auburn Street [the Window Shop's new location] because Mrs. Grant, a Viennese woman who had run a restaurant in Vienna, wanted to start one but could not get financing for it, and that building was available. It was owned by a Mr. Gravenstein of the bank on Dunster Street. Mr. Gravenstein was not a Jew but was very generous and very interested, and he rented us that building for $50 per month. We moved in three weeks before Christmas. We assembled enough stuff to make cookies; at this time there was Mrs. Schiffer and Mrs. Perutz [baking pastries]. In that three-week period, with the goods we had on consignment, we made a profit of $300."

Bessie Jones

"With a little more space and Mrs. Jones's volunteer but really professional management, the little shop sold more gifts and clothes, employed more refugees, and in the three weeks before Christmas, made a small profit.

"Mrs. Jones established standards and taught the consignors to make sweaters, skirts, and blouses that Americans would buy. She bought materials, clothes, and gift merchandise from refugees. She enlisted the support of more Harvard wives, who rallied as volunteers in the Shop and as purchasers. She still remembers a purchase of linen by one of the Harvard wives, which gave the Shop a real boost. But perhaps her most valuable contribution was the training of the Viennese teacher of languages and student of fine arts, Mary Mohrer, manager of the Window Shop Gift Shop."

Marion Muller

"Bessie Jones had enough retail experience to know that unless Mary Mohrer learned the business side of the operation she never would be able to be a good manager, nor would she be able to accomplish the things that her other talents were capable of achieving. So Bessie Jones insisted that Mary learn bookkeeping and stock control. She was able to recruit her own niece, Adele Bragar, who was a buyer at Gilchrist's and R. H. White's [large Boston department stores] to teach her. Mary was reluctant at first to accept the training."

Dorothy Dahl

A page from one of Mary Mohrer's ledgers, dated 1939.

"Bessie Jones is still in hysterics over my bookkeeping! I still think it was the smartest bookkeeping ever! I used three spindles: one for consignment merchandise, one for credits, and one for debits. And when I had time, I would transfer it all to a book."

Mary Mohrer

"While sales of cakes and pastries trebled gratifyingly, the high cost of the ingredients made it necessary to sacrifice the profit margin in order to keep prices within reason. Within six weeks of the move [to 102 Mount Auburn Street], the Gift Shop had disposed of almost $2,200 worth of goods, either made by refugees or handled by them as agents. One hundred refugees were being assisted in some way, and every possible means of including still more in the actual plan of work was considered. Volunteers performed a vital function serving teas and simple lunches, cleaning, and delivering orders."

Anonymous board member

"In 1940 it became evident that if the Shop was really to do the job it was setting out to do, namely, employ, retrain, and counsel refugees in the area, it was necessary to have a permanent organization. Accordingly, the Window Shop was incorporated as a charitable organization with Mrs. Clement A. Smith as its first president.... Our purpose was to give employment primarily to women who needed part-time work in order to help their husbands to resettle."

Anonymous board member

The following two excerpts are taken from the minutes of early board of directors' meetings, dated March 13, 1941, and April 7, 1941.
Articles of Incorporation, March 13, 1941
The Window Shop, Inc.

Purposes: To relieve and assist the poor and needy, including refugees from other countries, and in connection therewith to buy, sell, lease, and otherwise deal in or hold all sorts and kinds of personal property, to operate a Restaurant and Bakery, and in order to carry out the foregoing purposes, to own or lease real estate.

Incorporators: Margaret S. Blumgart, Alice Cope, Charles F. Dunbar, William Ehrlich, Helen M. Eisemann, Margaret Earhart Smith, F. Frank Vorenberg, Bessie Z. Jones.

Board: Margaret E. Smith, President; William Ehrlich, Treasurer; Charles F. Dunbar, Clerk/secretary.

[At its first meeting on that date, the board voted to employ a manager for the restaurant and bakery at a salary not to exceed $140 a month and to negotiate a lease at 102 Mount Auburn Street, rent not to exceed $275.]

[Second meeting of the board of directors, April 7, 1941]
Financial matters: The Window Shop has no lease or formal agreement at its present quarters. Consider other properties in Harvard Square, get statement in writing that would formalize a lease and promise a new lease.

Also discussed a financial program for the Window Shop and approaching potential donors to a financial appeal. Also funds for plant expansion with which goes program expansion, and funds to support operations until they pay their way.

"With the incorporation, the policy [of hiring large numbers of refugees], unchanged in principle, became clear-cut. With the business growing stronger daily, more people could be brought in, and new skills adapted to the community. Where there were no skills, there would be instruction. Thus by the program of training and by help given during the training period, the Window Shop could justify its existence.

"The policy of training and the situation of individuals needing help demanded a flexibility of organization not found in the usual commercial enterprise. Many workers manufactured articles in their own homes, meeting rigid requirements of quality. In the Shop, in the interest of benefiting more workers, one eight-hour job might be divided among a mother of small children unable to work full-time, a worker with just enough physical handicap to cause his rejection elsewhere, and a student with a full class schedule."

Anonymous board member

"Improvements in the dress line largely due to Mary Mohrer lead me to hope two things: that a similar improvement in the gift line might be achieved by a simplification and concentration of stock, and that the clothing business might be enlarged to include more and better services to the public.

"In the former case I do not have in mind the elimination of jewelry and small gifts, which, as it happens, move well, but rather the encouragement of our own workers, knitters, for example, to produce a less diversified stock of higher quality and larger quantity. This would improve our display and gradually give us a name for quality and usefulness in certain specialties which could be regarded as Window Shop specialties. Up to a point, diversification is good, but beyond that point it becomes merely messy and confusing. Up to now we have been often guided by the needs of workers themselves—and so we should be—and we have, I must acknowledge, attempted considerable restyling and direction in their work, but we have not gone as far in the process as we might. I think both the Window Shop and its workers could profit by an improvement in standards and a simplification of lines of goods."

Margaret Earhart Smith

Mrs. Baum prepares deviled eggs.

The Bakery/Tea Room

In the fall of 1939, Alice Perutz and Olga Schiffer, two refugee wives from Vienna, were making pastries in their homes and selling them to the Window Shop. Both women came from well-to-do Viennese families that employed cooks. While they had little experience in the kitchen, they definitely knew how good food should taste. Neither had ever worked outside her home, and they knew nothing about figuring costs or the complexities involved in selling food.

Nonetheless, their home-baked goods became a major attraction at the Window Shop, and after several months of "freelance" baking, Mrs. Perutz and Mrs. Schiffer became the Bakery's first staff members. During the Christmas 1939 season, sales of cakes and cookies tripled, while the profit margin dropped because of the high cost of the superior ingredients that the women were accustomed to buying.

Mrs. Perutz, who later remarried and became Mrs. Broch, reported that as she said good-bye to her family's cook, Marie, on the day she left Vienna for America, the woman thrust the family cookbook into her unwilling hands and said, "It might come in handy." It did, for the cookbook became the foundation of the Window Shop Restaurant.

Following the grand success of the Christmas sales of baked goods, Mrs. Nathan Gordon, the mother of Board Member Marion Bever, donated $300 to the Window Shop to help launch a Tea Room that both Mrs. Perutz and Mrs. Schiffer wanted to start. The Window Shop Tea Room opened in November 1939 in the basement of 102 Mount Auburn Street. At first, simple lunches were served. Before long, dinners were added—board members bought more card tables, more staff were hired, and soon a restaurant was on its way to occupying a special place in the hearts of its faithful patrons. Most of these early diners were Europeans, pleased to have found a cuisine that reminded them of home.

The executive committee decided that an American manager was needed for the fledgling restaurant, which prompted an irate letter from Mmes. Perutz and Schiffer: "There is no necessity and no room for any American manager, if only for the purpose of having the business run under an American flag." Apparently, xenophobic sentiment was running so high at the beginning of World War II that even the culturally diverse Window Shop was viewed with suspicion by some customers. "[Having lived] here for fifteen months and more, [we] have made so many friends that nobody doubts our feelings, our mindedness [*sic*], and our loyalty," Mrs. Perutz and Mrs. Schiffer proclaimed.[20]

Nonetheless, an American manager was hired for the Restaurant. ("A bad idea," observed Board Member Alice Cope.) Miss Frances Herrick of New York City was hired in March 1941 and was terminated two months later because of personality conflicts with the staff. In a letter to President Elsa Ulich, Board Member Margaret Smith painted a rosy picture: "This year under American management, the Tea Room's European clientele has practically disappeared [in favor of American customers]. Profits are up, and the landlord no longer threatens eviction." She pointed out that the Bakery must start figuring the cost of production more accurately, so that prices could be scaled accordingly, and added, "Mrs. Schiffer and Mrs. Perutz do not as yet agree to the importance of this step!"[21]

One of the hallmarks of the Window Shop was the spirit of cooperation among all members of the community, and the Restaurant was a key example. Refugees and board members worked side by side in the kitchen and the restaurant. Board members did anything that was needed—cooking, washing pots and pans, waitressing, hostessing, and selling pastries at the counter. Refugees cooked, baked, served as busboys and bus girls, and by the end of 1941, three refugee women were managers: Mrs. Perutz became the manager, with Mrs. Lotte Benfey and Mrs. Elisabeth Martens as her partners.

Board Member Bessie Jones managed the Gift and Dress Shop as a volunteer, with Mary Mohrer's help.

Voices

"Both Mrs. Schiffer and Mrs. Perutz began to make Viennese cookies and pastry in their homes in order to help support their families. They had learned to use the best materials—fresh sweet butter, fresh eggs, cream and nuts. They soon discovered, to their horror, the cost of their products in this country was prohibitive, and no one was able to pay their prices. Their efforts to use substitutes were not helped by those of their friends, who complained bitterly that the products did not taste the way they used to in Vienna. Americans, of course, did not know the difference. The cakes and cookies were so different, so delicious, and so good to look at that they were delighted with them, even though they were made with substitute ingredients."

Alice Cope

"One day in this difficult period of trial and error, two good friends descended the dark, steep stairs to the basement kitchen. They were Mr. and Mrs. Robert Jandorf, who had left Berlin in the early thirties when it was possible to bring with them some possessions. Hearing of the Window Shop and having sincere interest in European refugees, they had come to see what this Shop was doing. Mr. Jandorf talked with the two women, who were feeling depressed that morning. He told them how fortunate they were to have such jobs in Cambridge, with the backing of sympathetic people, and that they could set an example to other refugees by proving that by using their skills they could make a place for themselves in an American city.

"The next morning Mrs. Jandorf appeared with apron, having traveled from Brookline by streetcar, rolled up her sleeves, and did anything in the kitchen which needed to be done. The comfort of having a competent person who spoke their language and could teach them much that they needed to know restored their morale. And for more than a year Mrs. Jandorf continued her trek from Brookline every day."

Marion Muller

"I was asked to take over the management of the Tea Room, which it was a pleasure for me to do. The Tea Room met with great success during December, a success to be attributed first to the ability of Mrs. Perutz and Mrs. Schiffer in baking and catering, and secondly to the very favorable attitude of the local public, especially of a group of Cambridge women who have shown their profound concern in refugee problems ever since the Window Shop was opened. It was agreed that Mrs. Perutz and Mrs. Schiffer should receive a fixed salary of $12 a week and should divide any profit at the end of the month. It was fortunate that a profit was made, since the amount of work done and the time spent by both women was such that the salary of $12 a week would have been very inadequate. Their working hours during the whole month have been from eight or nine in the morning until ten in the evening, and inevitably they have had to work on Sundays as well."

Erna Jandorf

"Mrs. Percy Bridgman [a volunteer] and I both went [to Boston] to testify for Mary's [Mohrer] citizenship. [Then] Mrs. Bridgman and I went to a wholesale furniture store and bought four easy chairs for $6 apiece. We went to Cooley China Shop and bought four of those folding tables to serve tea with the cookies the women baked. By that time, Margaret Smith had come into the enterprise. Her husband was a pediatrician. Marg was very restless and very philanthropic and wanted to do something. Since giving me that $150 check, she had gotten deeply involved in helping refugees in Cambridge. She offered to pay for remodeling the Window Shop and what eventually became the Restaurant—the left side of it became a Tea Room and the right side of it a shop. The basement was going to be the kitchen. We probably violated every sanitary rule in the code. We bought a secondhand sink and a secondhand stove, and that's what we started the Tea Room with."

Bessie Jones

"The business at Mount Auburn Street was somewhat unusual because we couldn't cook there. The kitchen was over on Willard Street, across from the Cambridge Skating Club. My mother sent her chauffeur down. Now it was a restaurant, not a bakery any more. Mary [Mohrer] did sell food in that shop, food that people brought in. But now we had a place where we could sell our bakery goods, and also run a limited restaurant. It was only open for lunch.... I was on the crew that brought the food from Willard Street. We had a slew of people with station wagons, and we'd go back and forth, back and forth! Things had to be kept hot, so that the food was hot when it was served.

"At that time there were two women in the kitchen: Mrs. Schiffer and Mrs. Broch (she was Mrs. Perutz then). They were the cooks there. An unlikelier pair you never saw in your life! Mrs. Schiffer was kind of a prickly, upper middle class Jewish lady whose husband was [a student] at the Harvard Law School and who had two children here, and who worked very hard, but who always felt, I think, that it was somewhat beneath her. But she kept right at it. Mrs. Schiffer was always trying to be a lady on the side, whereas Mrs. Broch would just roll up her sleeves. She didn't care. She was just working hard, and she was always a lady anyway. They were quite different."

Marion Bever

"Please do not underestimate the fact that this little place [the Tea Room] has become a matter of very personal relationships between customers and employees. I who have worked there have heard this expressed over and over."

Undated letter from Elsa Ulich to the executive committee

"The accommodations were neither stylish nor comfortable. There was a friendly rat named 'Charlie' who came and went between kitchen and dining room, to the consternation and humiliation of Mrs. Perutz. The customers were not so upset, and one told Mrs. Perutz that she shouldn't be … everyone had such problems once in a while! Mrs. Perutz was not happy. Another wonderful board member, Mrs. Robert Jandorf, volunteered to help get the Restaurant-Bakery on an even keel. At one point, the board decided that what was needed was an American-trained manager. Several were tried. That idea was a disaster."

Alice Cope

"Presently there were five refugee cooks working in the tiny, ill-equipped kitchen, and instead of volunteers bringing the food from the basement and serving it in the little lunchroom upstairs, refugee waitresses were employed. I asked Professor Jaeger the other day, lunching at the Window Shop as he usually does, if he lunched at the Shop in those early days. 'Yes,' he said with his whimsical smile, 'and they had few tables, so they placed us beside very interesting people.'"

Marion Muller

"Reorganization has not only become necessary in the Shop and the kitchen, but in the committee itself. And while businessmen and lawyers tried to solve the problems concerning legal and business matters of the future of the Shop, the Shop had to go on with its daily routine. Therefore a small committee had been set up within the committee. Suggestions [for improving the Shop's routine] were:

- Meals should be planned sometime in advance.

- A special "Schnitzel" day should be fixed and be advertised on the menu.

- Catering services should be increased.

- Part of the staff could have luncheon before noon, eating the previous day's food; the rest after customers had gone and the kitchen was clean.

- The following items were needed: more tablecloths; coat and hat rack and umbrella stand for the Shop; a drawer for the kitchen.

- All customers should be greeted in a friendly way by whoever is at hand."

Meeting of board subcommittee, Feb. 5, 1940

"Every Monday Marg Smith and I would turn up at Mount Auburn Street and put out the trash. That was our job. In the earliest days, I worked in the Shop, helping Mary. We did displays, I sold, I did anything she asked me to do. I worked very hard at the Shop. When the zoning was changed, we were able to move the restaurant to the basement of this building. The war was on the way, too. It was all very scary at this time. We wondered how people would feel about refugees, particularly Germans. Actually in Cambridge, I don't think we ever had any difficulty. It's kind of a magic place for that kind of thing anyway. At any rate, once the food was cooked downstairs in the basement, it made a big difference. There was this narrow stairway. I can remember carrying trays up and down. I was a waitress then. Mary could find plenty of people to work in the Shop. It was much harder to get help for the Restaurant. We even had a bakery counter at that time, downstairs in the basement. I used to man the Bakery. It was mostly orders. We didn't have a refrigerator.

"The Restaurant was wild! It brought a lot of people into the Shop, and the Shop from the beginning was the moneymaker—right from the start. The Shop could operate with one paid worker, with volunteer help. For years that's all we had. The Restaurant needed cooks, bakers, waitresses, a head waiter; we needed a lot more help. And actually, of course, we helped a great many more people."

Marion Bever

"Refugees came to the Restaurant [as customers]. There was Professor von Mises and Professor Jaeger,[22] who came because they wanted some of that Austrian food. After Christmas, the two women [Broch and Schiffer] wanted to serve lunches. We got some card tables, and that was what we served lunches on. And then they wanted to serve dinner, and they did. We would take the little tea tables down and set up the card tables—and that is what started the Restaurant."

Bessie Jones

"The Cambridge community supported the enterprise—they bought the tea and they bought gifts there. The community did all the work."

Mary Mohrer

"This branch of the business, which ran at a deficit of over $2,000 last year, has pulled out of the red to the point where it is meeting day-to-day operating costs, including the manager's salary. It is not doing more than this, however, or very little more, chiefly because in the present quarters it has not room to grow. Using the downstairs room as we at present propose doing seems a logical next step, but not the last one which we shall be called upon to take, for it leaves us with a future space problem....

"In general, with regard to both branches of the Shop, I would hope that we might revise wages upward at least in the more important and responsible jobs."

Margaret Smith

"I would say what made the Restaurant successful in the first place was the food. The food was different, totally different, and the people loved it. I have to say I am not Viennese, and I loved it myself. This Viennese salad with two stuffed eggs on it and all raw salad, raw cabbage, potato salad, two stuffed eggs, went like hotcakes, every lunchtime! It was healthy—it was very healthy—and it tasted so good. It was famous. They were all Mrs. Broch's recipes. And then we had, of course, *Wiener Schnitzel*, a veal cutlet fried in deep fat, and it tasted wonderful. Those things we just loved. And there were a lot of Viennese items which we who came from Germany did not know before, because they never served them in German restaurants. And she brought all these recipes, and the food was different, and that's what the attraction was. That was what people loved. And it was nicer than an ordinary restaurant because they knew who we were—that we had come from nice families; people were aware of that, and that made a little difference to us."

Elisabeth Martens

Waitress takes orders in the Window Shop Restaurant.

Two

Growth and Success: The Move to Brattle Street

When Elsa Brändström Ulich became president of the Window Shop in the fall of 1942, she believed that the Restaurant and Bakery could be successful. There was nothing like it in Harvard Square, and a loyal customer base had been established. She convinced the board that refugees were now ready to be managers. Alice Perutz, who had been with the shop since the fall of 1939, first as the baker of delicious pastries and then as a cook, had taken cooking courses in the summers, helped run a restaurant, and managed the kitchen of a summer hotel. Now she would manage the kitchen, and Mrs. Ulich would direct the waitresses.

Three months later the Restaurant showed a small profit. From October 15, 1942, until March 15, 1943, Mrs. Ulich herself took the job of hostess for luncheons after an employee left. Mr. Zuntz, who had owned the Zuntz Coffee Houses in Germany and who managed the Goodwill House in Groton, was then hired as host both for lunches and dinners. In the spring of 1943, Mrs. Ulich said, "There is no place in Cambridge where people are so aware of the refugee spirit as the Window Shop, and there is no doubt we are creating good feeling toward refugees. Many customers take a great personal interest in the fate of individual refugees."

The Window Shop operated during World War II, when some supplies were scarce, and prices of the best ingredients increased. It became difficult for the managers to make a profit while food costs soared, and they were faced with the problem of maintaining the quality of their unique products.

The executive committee asked the Office of Price Administration for permission to raise the price ceilings in the Restaurant and Gift Shop to make it possible to maintain a fair profit. With the approval of the War Labor Board, the executive committee also increased wages in the Restaurant.

In March 1945, the financial report was glowing. The managers of the Gift Shop and Restaurant were both pleased, but "a little embarrassed" and amazed by the extraordinary growth and success of the Window Shop. "At lunch, the tables are filled three and a half times," Mrs. Perutz reported modestly.

With financial stability came a crisis. Unexpectedly, conflicts arose with the landlord at 102 Mount Auburn Street, who had received numerous complaints from tenants in the building about the cooking odors emanating from the basement kitchen. The Cambridge Board of Health was called in, and finally the landlord asked the executive committee to find new quarters.

Late in 1946 the landlord decided not to renew the Window Shop's lease. Lady Luck came forward in the form of a deliveryman who told Mrs. Perutz (who was now Mrs. Broch) that the Cock Horse Restaurant in the Dexter Pratt House on Brattle Street was for sale. He suggested that the Window Shop buy it. In no time, she, Board President Elsa Brändström Ulich, and Mary Mohrer inspected the premises and convinced the board that the move would be a good one.

The old Federal-style house was probably built in 1811 by Torrey Hancock, owner of a blacksmith's shop on the corner of Story Street. Henry Wadsworth Longfellow wrote the poem, "The Village Blacksmith," in 1839, when the house belonged to his friend, Dexter Pratt. It saw a good deal of history through its old windows, and at one time reportedly housed a glue factory in its shed.

"It was in great disrepair, full of vermin and rats, and in many places falling apart," said Alice Cope about the building in a talk in October 1984.

Soon all the board members took a look and saw the larger space and the charm of the old house and garden "with the glorious wisteria over the door." All agreed that this should be the Window Shop's new home, but where would the money come from to buy and restore the property? There was hesitation, as one board member wrote, in "agreeing to sink our present and future profits in bricks and mortar rather than using them to help needy refugees."

But doubts were eased, and after a special meeting of the board of directors in March 1946, Mrs. Ulich met with George Macomber, president of the Cambridge Trust Company, who promised her a mortgage. The board had decided that $40,000 would be needed to restore the old house and install the necessary equipment for the Gift and Dress Shop and the Restaurant. That amount would be borrowed from board members and some of their generous friends, with the understanding that all funds would be repaid within ten years. The board voted to proceed. As members filed out of the meeting, Alice Cope reports that a board member turned to her and said, "I don't know why we had to have a meeting. Mrs. Ulich would never have accepted anything but 'Yes'!"

The restoration of the house was an enormous challenge, and staying within the budget was difficult. The project was supervised by architect and board member Elizabeth Aub. After all the pitfalls and headaches that invariably accompany a project of this scope were overcome, the restoration was finished, and with everyone's help, staff and board members alike, the Window Shop moved to Brattle Street in March 1947.

"We had a beautiful day for the opening," reported Alice Cope, "and crowds of our friends and neighbors inspected every corner. During the refreshments, we ran out of cream. I went across to Sage's Market to get some more and ran into old Mr. Sage. I asked him whether he had been over to see our new shop. 'No, I haven't,' he answered, 'but I hear that you ladies have done it again.' In one short sentence, Mr. Sage said what many people thought." The ladies had done it again, thanks to the wide support of the community—from the bank president to friends of the board—and thanks to "the determination of every Window Shop worker and board member," said Mrs. Cope.

With the larger space on Brattle Street, the Window Shop could employ almost twice as many people as before. They were needed because customers streamed in, delighted with the attractively displayed giftware and dresses and the Old World elegance of Viennese pastries with coffee *mit Schlag* [with whipped cream]. After six months on Brattle Street, profits were up, spirits were high, and the hardworking managers—Mary Mohrer and Alice Broch—finally received well-earned, if modest, raises. In the fall of 1947, Mrs. Ulich was ill, but she still managed the Window Shop from her bed. She died on March 28, 1948.

In the summer, customers enjoyed their meals under the gay umbrellas in the courtyard, an experience thought to be the first outdoor dining in Cambridge. But in the fall and winter, with the courtyard empty of tables, it was not obvious that there was a restaurant. Mary Mohrer asked Gyorgy Kepes,[23] an artist from Hungary, to design a logo for the new building. He created the cock horse (a rocking horse) design that was used on stationery and place mats, and most famously, the sign on Brattle Street.

In 1954, the Window Shop Restaurant earned recognition in *A Guide to Distinctive Dining: Recipes from Famous Restaurants in America*.[24] Luncheon was listed as "from $.95, dinner from $1.85."

Voices

"There has been no rise in prices during the last six months. We have cut out a few dishes which were too expensive. It is a great strain for us to continue with our old prices, when for instance, one of our most important ingredients—nuts—have risen from 42 cents to 90 cents a pound, mushrooms from $1 to $1.75....

"Today we had 120 people for lunch, 90 upstairs, 30 downstairs, which means that every table has been used three times between twelve and two o'clock. Also fifty-one dinner guests yesterday—we reached our capacity at lunch and at dinner."

Elsa Brändström Ulich Report to board, November 23, 1943

"During the war, as rationing and price-fixing came into effect, a whole new bag of troubles fell on the small group. It was then that the spirit of the Window Shop and of its workers overcame each problem. Workers would bring their own small ration of butter and sugar and coffee. The delivery men from the wholesalers brought a pound of something beyond the ration. Volunteers squeezed a little from their family ration. Miraculously, it sometimes seemed, the whole Shop prospered."

Alice Cope

"Then there was the business of modifying the original European recipes to fit wartime availabilities and, I suppose, American tastes. I remember Mother [Alice Cope] talking with Mrs. Broch about what they could substitute for real butter and cream; she explained to us what the 'real thing' was like, if you had it in Europe. I think there was some doubt in the kitchen that downgrading to margarine and whatever would be possible."

Eliza Cope Harrison

"We have had to train new people, since several of our experienced workers have left and have been replaced with unskilled ones. This, of course, increases the burden on Mrs. Perutz. She is still receiving only $30 a week, having refused a raise in salary unless the three other chief cooks received one."

Elsa Brändström Ulich

"We were the first place in the city of Cambridge to employ black women. That started because of Mrs. Broch. They needed extra help in the kitchen, and those poor women were begging for work. Mrs. Broch was responsible for hiring the first black women who came. She would never let us call her the boss, but that's when Elsa [Ulich] came in and said, 'You know, every team has to have a leader, because everyone is not going to get along all the time perfectly.' It was interesting because the kitchen and the restaurant and the bakery had many more workers than ever before. Alice Broch was past master at finding part-time workers. She started with the waitresses; that was easy. They could come in for one meal. Then the mothers of children who were in school would come and work in the mornings and through lunch, and they'd be home in time for the children.

"The blacks were coming to work for practically nothing. It was one of the things that Elsa didn't really understand. She thought it was all right to pay the blacks less than we paid the whites. She certainly didn't treat them differently. They were human beings, and that was all she cared about. They loved her, but I think it never entered her head that there was something very wrong about having an absolutely first-class black cook being paid about half of what an absolutely first-class refugee cook was being paid. But once it was laid out on the table, everybody saw that it was wrong. It was a very uncomfortable time."

Alice Cope

"During the war, when immigration was almost at a standstill, it was decided to employ Americans. Many of these were Negroes. We soon found that our New Americans (we tried very hard to stop using the term 'refugee') learned more quickly and adapted to their new life better when they worked with American-born. The European has no prejudice in regard to Negroes so that for the first time in many of their lives, Negroes found themselves on equal terms with their fellow workers. This has been a wonderful experience for all concerned, and some of our workers who are most devoted to the ideals and principles of the Window Shop are found among our Negro employees."

Anonymous board member

"The only African American woman that I remember was Martha Washington. She and her two children, if I remember correctly, spent a summer with us [the Aub family] in Rhode Island, and my mother was not completely unprejudiced, but I think that Martha Washington did the cooking. Her kids had a nice vacation in the country, but I don't think she was completely free to do what she wanted to do. That was a nice summer, and the kids were nice kids. I think she was the only non-refugee there."

Nancy Aub Gleason

"The move to Brattle Street was made. As the years went by, many additions and changes were made within the building, but the structure of the old house with its glorious wisteria vine over the front door was kept unchanged. The staircase, though graceful and lovely, was a burden for many [in the Restaurant], but even this was overcome. The young went upstairs, the less young stayed down. The garden in summer was an oasis in a crowded city."

Alice Cope

"I think the Window Shop started eating outdoors in Cambridge—now everybody who has two inches of sidewalk puts two tables out, and I think we were the first. It was very European, and our business was so dependent on the weather. How Mrs. Broch, Elisabeth Martens, and Mrs. Benfey ran that restaurant was absolutely extraordinary. I learned one thing. You can run a restaurant very well, but you can also lose money very fast. Financially we did very well until the beginning of the sixties. We were employing more and more people.

"The only thing I hated about the Window Shop was when I was asked occasionally to be a hostess. I don't know how people can be hostesses in restaurants, because all your friends come up and say, 'All right, why don't you seat me there?' 'Well, I can't because that's reserved.' I hated it! I loved selling in the Gift Shop, but I hated being a hostess!"

Hedy Sturges

"A few figures show how much the whole Shop grew. From December 1942 to December 1946, the cash surplus grew from around $11,000 to almost $44,000. In 1942 the salary figure was about $8,400; in 1967 it was $241,000. In the peak years, from 75 to 110 people were employed in the entire Shop, depending on the time of year, and close to 1,000 were guided in one way or another to a solution of their problems. Each department sustained the other. Depending on the weather and time of year, from 300 to 800 people came into the building each day."

Alice Cope

"On a peer level the waitresses and occasional waiter all became good friends, spending free time together. Even though we worked hard carrying heavy trays over the picturesque but not foot-friendly bricks of the Village Blacksmith's patio, we did have a lot of fun.... Special events were celebrated in the 'party room.' As waitresses, we always loved to be assigned to the party room because the work wasn't nearly as demanding as the public dining rooms, and then there was always a feast of delicious leftovers when all the guests went home....

"As winter approached in the fall of 1948, we still lived in a cold-water flat with inadequate heat. One of the bakery employees at the Window Shop connected us to her landlady, and we were able to rent an apartment in the building in which she lived at a rental we could afford. This was the first adequate housing we had since we left Vienna in 1938. The landlady rented to us because of the Window Shop connection, which she trusted. Since there were almost no apartments to be had in Cambridge at an affordable rental, this offer in itself was quite remarkable. It was in this apartment that our Window Shop-catered wedding reception took place forty-nine years ago. My parents continued to live there for many years and eventually moved to another apartment again owned by the same landlady."

Nadia Ehrlich Finkelstein

"[After the war], refugees, now called Displaced Persons, were coming to the Window Shop for work, advice and financial help. A member of the board, Mr. Walter Bieringer, was chairman of the Boston Committee in charge of DPs, as he had been chairman of the Boston Refugee Committee when the Window Shop began. He kept us informed of the situation and urged us to employ some of the people who were most difficult to place. The managers were spending so much time interviewing, finding jobs when possible, and counseling these distressed, bewildered people that they had to be relieved. For several months one of the executive committee was engaged to give five mornings a week to this work. Eventually the president [Alice Cope] undertook the task as a full-time volunteer with an office and secretary. Her interests and her talents fitted her for this work, and since she was there every day, the managers and employees also could confer with her."

Marion Muller

"I had never in my life been a waitress. I was a nurse. I learned from one of the women there, Ursula Loewy, also from Germany.... But you do have to learn different customs. Where I came from in Germany, people were served hot food, they ate it, and then they had their conversation. When they put their knife and fork down, that means they were done. Well, I wanted to be efficient, and the moment somebody put their knife and fork down, I grabbed their plates! Then Mrs. Benfey very politely said to me that 'This is not the way. Would you please let them finish?'

"I had a busboy who was a student of theology, and we got along very well. One day at Harvard graduation, there he comes with his mother, specially looking for me. He had to introduce his boss—I was his boss! Later on I met him somewhere, and he was a Reverend ... my busboy!"

Tamar Wurmfeld

"Our [board members'] children had jobs there in the summertime. Both of mine [did]—one was a waitress or whatever and the other was a busboy. They still remember all the discipline from Mrs. Benfey! They were treated the same way as all the staff—it was very good for them."

Hedy Sturges

"Jana Hnilicka, a young student, worked in the Gift Shop one summer. Her family had come from Czechoslovakia in the early 1950s. Her father was a professor at MIT, and they lived on a farm in Concord [fifteen miles northwest of Cambridge]. On her first day at work, Jana had left her wallet at home. She didn't feel comfortable enough to ask anyone to lend her money for the train home. So she took off her shoes and walked home!"

Ilse Heyman

Ilse Heyman and Mary Mohrer at the display case.

Mary Mohrer's Gift and Dress Shop

By 1949, ten years after the Window Shop's rather humble beginnings, the Gift and Dress Shop had built a loyal customer base among the affluent, influential, and discerning residents of Cambridge and Greater Boston and was enjoying its first financial success.

The success of the Gift and Dress Shop is attributable in large part to Mary Mohrer, who became its manager in 1942. Her art background, her exquisite taste, her gift for design, her training in business practices under Bessie Jones, and her intuitive interest in people all contributed to her achievement in making the Window Shop the place to shop for unique and tasteful merchandise. The small space, first on Mount Auburn Street and then on Brattle Street, was artistically decorated and stocked with glassware, pottery, casserole dishes, wooden bowls, fabrics, jewelry, and women's clothing—all personally selected by Mary. The staff, led by assistant manager Ilse Heyman, lavished attention on the customers, many of whom became personal friends as well as loyal clients, who returned again and again to see what Mary had brought back from her buying trips around the world.

The Window Shop became a showcase for artisans, craftspeople, and design-ers, and Mary nurtured all of them. Famed painter Albert Alcalay, for example, who lived in hiding in Italy during World War II, came to Boston after the war and eventually taught at Harvard's Carpenter Center. Mary immediately saw his talent and introduced him to some of her wealthier customers. He used to joke, "I couldn't have had a better agent than Mary Mohrer."

Lore Kadden Lindenfeld, who became a celebrated weaver and textile designer, came to the Window Shop as a young student. Her family fled Germany in 1937 and lived in Holland for two years. Lore had studied fashion design in Dusseldorf, Germany, and in Holland she was a seamstress in a work-shop that made clothes for Queen Wilhelmina of the Netherlands. In 1939, the Kadden family came to the Boston area, and Lore found employment at the Window Shop as Mary Mohrer's first assistant in the Gift and Dress Shop. With a small stipend from the Shop's Assistance Fund, Lore was able to attend Black Mountain College, where she studied design with artists Josef and Anni Albers. After graduating from Black Mountain in Weaving and Textile Design in August 1948, Lore Kadden moved to New York City and worked as a successful designer in several textile companies. She later became an independent weaver whose hangings have been exhibited in many galleries, and she continues her work today as a fiber artist.

Mary Mohrer had an unerring gift for searching out craftspeople all over the world for the benefit of her customers back in Cambridge. She faithfully main-tained her contacts and friendships with artisans on several continents. "My con-tact with the wife of our then-ambassador in Togo, Africa, resulted in a cooperation which lasted as long as her husband was stationed there," she recalled. "I still remember the wonderful colors and embroideries of those gar-ments." From Senegal, Mary Mohrer brought necklaces made of old beads, bracelets of horn, ebony, and silver—jewelry never seen before in the United States.

In Jerusalem, on a buying trip, she found a nonprofit organization called Lifeline for the Aged. It hired elderly men and women to string clay beads in nat-ural colors to make necklaces and earrings. It was said that the length of the neck-laces was determined by the time between cigarette breaks for the men. In the old section of Jerusalem, she met two Israeli glassblowers whose exquisite bowls and vases rivaled the best Venetian glass. On the Greek island of Mykonos, Mary met a woman called Vinoula who wove woolen place mats, table runners, and Greek bags in vibrant colors and unique designs. In Athens, she found weavers who made special fabrics for skirts and dresses to be sold in the Window Shop. One day, her own infallible sense of style prompted her to suggest a change in a small toy factory in Greece: "My changing the tail of a wooden horse from silk to rope resulted in a sale of five thousand pieces, which were shipped to Germany."

Beautiful hand-blocked silk scarves made by Anne Gaposchkin, the daughter-in-law of famed Harvard astronomer Cecilia Payne-Gaposchkin, and silk batik scarves designed by an Israeli woman named Yoval were sold at the Window Shop before they were seen in any of the fine stores in the Boston area.

Hand-enameled jewelry, ash trays, and platters designed and made by Celia Somervell, Mary Mohrer's sister, were popular items in the shop. Mrs. Somervell, who had studied art at the *Kunstakademie* in Vienna before the family fled, worked in oils and watercolors, and her work was exhibited in the Boston area.

All these items from a variety of cultures and traditions found their way back to Cambridge with Mary Mohrer. Harvard Square had never seen anything like the Gift Shop. It drew customers like a magnet. Before or after shopping, customers (mostly women) would very likely have coffee and pastry or lunch at the adjacent Restaurant. Together, the Gift and Dress Shop and the Restaurant/Bakery prospered. Although there were many problems in running the enterprise, especially while the United States was at war, the late 1940s through the mid-1960s marked the Window Shop's best years.

Voices

"In 1947, I hired Ilse Heyman, who became my assistant, after she had an anti-Semitic experience in a dress factory in Boston. She had come to the United States six months earlier after spending two and a half years in German slave labor and concentration camps. Later, I was looking for help, and I wanted to find somebody who would fit into the group. A German girl applied for the job. I looked at her and said, 'I'll be very frank with you. Many of the people who work here have been in concentration camps. Many of them have sores and wounds that are very fresh. I don't think you would be happy here, and I think it would create great turmoil in my group. I don't think I can hire you.' She looked at me and said, 'But I was a little girl then.' It was sad. But I did not hire her."

Mary Mohrer

"I was scared stiff of having a job as a salesperson. I was shy, I had no self-confidence, I had to talk to people, and Mary did that beautifully, but I had a very hard time. But meanwhile, they were preparing to move to Brattle Street, and Mary was most of the time out of the building talking with architects, so I had to struggle to write out a sales slip, to know the difference between charge and cash—what did I know of that? So I was lucky that I knew the bookkeeper upstairs, Mrs. [Ruth] Welland, and I could ask her.

"My first customers were as shy as I was, but I will never forget the first young woman. Her husband was at MIT, she had just become pregnant, and they had to go to a dance, and she didn't want the pregnancy to show. So we made her a long skirt and a blouse, and she was delighted. And she became a friend, because they then became the directors of the Experiment in International Living, they went to Holland, they visited my cousin there. And years later she came with her daughter who went to Radcliffe. So the friendships through the Window Shop were very, very important.

"After a while I began to be more comfortable with customers and learned the expressions I didn't know—different names of glasses—old-fashioneds. A man came in and asked, 'Do you have old-fashioneds?' and I wanted to say, 'But look around you, this is such a modern store.' Luckily I didn't say anything, but I looked at Mary, and Mary went like this [gestures], and the man saw the glasses and said, 'Of course you have old-fashioneds.' So when I trained new people, and I trained many of them, one of the first things I did was go to the glasses, and I made sure they knew what they all were for."

Ilse Heyman

"One day Mrs. Epstein of the Christian Committee for Refugees in Cambridge asked me to meet the Wallachs in their apartment in Woodside, Queens. Mr. Wallach came from Munich, where he established the Wallach House for Folk Art. There he created hand-blocked traditional designs, fabrics, costumes, etc. In 1938, when the Nazis confiscated his business, Mr. and Mrs. Wallach came to New York. The Refugee Committee lent them some money so they could buy linen; they rented a printer's table and a dye kitchen for very minimal rent and started to produce their authentic designs in hand-blocked linens. There, in their fourth-floor apartment, we discussed merchandising. The Window Shop gave Wallach a big display and sold his linens. When Mrs. Roosevelt came to a dinner party given in her honor at the Window Shop, we presented her with the most beautiful of his tablecloths."

Mary Mohrer

"We had Mrs. Heppner, who worked at home and made skirts, short or long. We gave her the measurements; we had some very nice fabrics. And we had another woman, Mrs. Bullerwell, an American, who made blouses at home. Mrs. Heppner was German, and she, with her friend—they were two lovely, mature women—had obviously never done anything like that in Germany, but for many years we worked with them. Once the dirndl craze began, people would come in, and I would take measurements and send them to Alice Boehm [the Window Shop dressmaker].

"We had fabric samples. In the summer we had summer fabrics that were mostly Wallach fabrics, and in the winter we had wool—black and green. The dirndls all had names—Norwegian, Austrian, whatever—and so I would write an order for dirndl such and such, take the measurements, and it was made. Before I came, I think Mary had lots of traumas with people who wanted complicated things done, like wedding dresses, and people weren't equipped to do it well, and it was nightmarish. But once Alice Boehm was back in town (she went to Seattle for a while), then it worked.

"After a while people didn't want dirndls any more, and the skirts and blouses—you could buy them cheaper and ready-made. We couldn't pay the workers enough. It just wasn't worth it. Alice Boehm by that time was very well established. She didn't need the dirndls any more, although there were still some people, like Anna Freud, who insisted on long dirndls. She worked through her friend, the analyst Grete Bibring, who lived in Cambridge and was a customer of ours.

"By the time we moved to Brattle Street, Mary had bought ready-made skirts, blouses, coats, and jackets. We had suits, we had more expensive things, and we had Henry Rosenfeld, which, you know, was an $11.95 dress, $14.95 dress, I mean inexpensive. But we still made blouses—I still gave orders to Alice Boehm and to Mrs. Bullerwell."

Ilse Heyman

"I was a waitress in the Restaurant, and one day Mary Mohrer [from the Gift Shop] came and asked if I would like to help them with packing the packages that they were mailing out. And these were all things I could do while the kids were in kindergarten. I could make my own hours and so on. In the beginning we used boxes and God knows what, and slowly I got that organized. We ordered the right-size boxes, we ordered excelsior [packing material], and then I took these boxes—we had a little red wagon that somebody brought, and then we got bigger so we ordered one of those laundry rollers that big laundries have—and I rolled this along the street. The post office had stairs, and I made friends with the people at the post office, and they let me come in the back door where there were no stairs. We had very good treatment there. At Christmas we made a big cake for everybody [at the post office]."

Tamar Wurmfeld

"I remember when working at the Window Shop I met a young potter who sold her wares at astonishingly low prices. When I asked her whether she had figured electricity, heat, light, and breakage, in addition to time and clay, she was surprised. She said that she never thought of all that, and that she did not 'need so much money.' She did raise her prices and met no resistance. However, when her first shipment arrived at the Window Shop, she had added two dozen beautiful small pots free of charge to make up for possible breakage in transit....

"The Window Shop was not only an outlet for the craftsmen here and abroad. We were consultants. We taught the craftsmen where to buy their materials, how to price their wares, and where to find additional outlets. We could not sell paintings, but we could advise newly arrived painters where to go for contacts."

Mary Mohrer

"We grew rapidly, and we needed even more help, so we had very quickly part-time help, certainly at Christmas, certainly in the summer, and somehow the Window Shop made us all feel that we were family. The cook came out one day and yelled across the whole Shop, 'Tell the baby her lunch is ready!' Well, I was the baby because I was so much younger than everybody else. It certainly was nice."

Ilse Heyman

"I was in the back packing one day, before Christmas it must have been, I think it was '54, and Ilse comes running in and says, 'Tamar, can you help us?'

"'Help what?'

"'Well, there's a lady in the fitting room, and she's trying on a coat.'

"I go; I speak to her very politely. I haven't the slightest notion about selling and certainly not selling fashion. I wasn't brought up to like that. It was an alpaca-lined tweed coat, the price was $75, and Mrs. Ryerson (she was later my customer for years, we loved each other) said, 'I'll take it.' And I nearly passed out! I ran to Ilse and said, 'Ilse, what do I do now? She said she takes it!'

"She said, 'You'll charge it.' 'What's a charge?' I said.

"So Ilse was a great help, and she knew the name of everybody, and so she wrote it out, Mrs. Ryerson, and she had no time even to teach me. Well, this was the beginning of my career working at the Window Shop!

"As we had a little time afterwards, I was introduced to the various kinds of materials, different types of glasses—I didn't know what's an old-fashioned, a double old-fashioned, and so on—that was fine. At the same time I unpacked everything that was shipped and organized it, and we were a good team together, a very good team together."

Tamar Wurmfeld

"For all the years that the Window Shop existed, [Board Member] Lillian Cohan Levin was an enthusiastic supporter of the enterprise, and when we moved to Brattle Street, she was a volunteer salesperson in the Gift and Dress Shop at every holiday season. She loved those beautiful items and clothes, and she must have increased total holiday sales by an identifiable percentage, for who could possibly say no to Lil?"

Dorothy Dahl

"Lil Cohan was one of the most generous people there was. Once a year she had a big sale. All year 'round she bought silver, jewelry, and unusual items and resold them. Half the money went to the Window Shop Scholarship Fund and half to Hadassah. She did this every year, and she made a lot of money, but she also worked at the Window Shop. She had family in retailing, and she came with suitcases of clothes. At the end of the Christmas season one year, her husband came with champagne and pastry that she had made. There was such generosity. And at Christmastime she brought in all her rich friends. Sometimes she would be a problem because she would interrupt what you were doing, and she needed immediate help! But she brought in a lot of business. She was a dear lady, one of the nicest volunteers we had."

Ilse Heyman

"In Miss Mohrer's department there are relatively few employees ... but she helps many people whose names never appear on our payroll. By designing clothes and other salable articles to be made at home, she has helped support many people who are unable to go out to work. Some have eventually started their own businesses."

Elizabeth Aub

"The restaurant business was, in general, a bit more hectic, I would say. But in the Window Shop the two really big things were the Christmas season, and you prepared for that months ahead, and then the graduation and wedding season. I had to learn what it means to be registered for wedding gifts, and all these things seemed so strange, you know, but you learn as you go along, and if you have nice people with you, then that helps.

"Now Mary was a born teacher, absolutely. And Ilse was really the one who did the most, I must say, because Ilse was much more patient, but in the beginning she was very reserved, until she got to know me, very reserved, and I respected that. But we were just very different. We came every morning, a quarter of an hour earlier, at quarter to nine, and we dusted everything. And while we dusted we chatted. And we had there one girl—she was French, her husband was a philosophy student, a graduate student—and Marie [Swanson] was a bit crazy, but fun. And she, of course, talked. But Ilse liked to be quiet at this time, so everybody respected that. And Marie, crazy as she was, she dusted this big carving set, and all of a sudden she said, 'I'm going to do hara-kiri!' And she takes the sharp knife and literally slits her belly. We went into the bathroom, and put a Band-Aid on it. It wasn't ... a little blood was shed, but this is the kind of thing that happened!"

Tamar Wurmfeld

"Marie was a French Resistance fighter. She was a little bit of a thing, fiery dark eyes, lots of makeup, but she was a Parisian. She had fought with the Irgun in Palestine and was a real rabble-rouser. We had lots of fun with her. She was very outspoken, and she spoke with this wonderful French accent."

Ilse Heyman

"One day in New York I saw a very beautiful, hand-enameled bracelet. I was determined to find out who the craftsman was. With much perseverance I found Doris Hall who, at that time, lived in Cleveland, Ohio. She had received many awards but had not shown [her work] in the East. We gave her a display, provided exposure, and a new outlet for her and added prestige for the Window Shop. My friendship with her and her very talented husband, Kalman Kubinyi, lasted for many years through correspondence only. Later, when she and her family moved to Massachusetts, our friendship was cemented for life."

Mary Mohrer

"Most board members took turns volunteering in the Gift Shop when extra help was needed. They would wait on their friends and acquaintances and help them choose the right things. Even more stimulating were the visitors and tourists who came in droves to have a meal and buy something. The Shop's reputation had spread farther than anyone had imagined....

"While I was in high school and college, I worked in the Gift Shop during the Christmas rush and in June during the wedding season. I helped customers and did all the gift wrapping. I learned to wrap something in three minutes—you couldn't take any longer than that. I was terribly proud to be there, and since I was interested in human behavior, I found the job endlessly entertaining. For instance, it was there that I discovered how helpless men can be when it comes to gift buying, especially for their wives and daughters. As Christmas loomed, desperate husbands and fathers would surge into the Shop, having left their least favorite task until the zero hour—and gratefully accept all the guidance we could give them. Other cherished moments include going upstairs to Mr. Martens's office to get paid. He'd hand me a long, skinny manila envelope with my hours written on it. Sometimes it was quite heavy, since it contained cash.

"Mary Mohrer and Ilse Heyman were terrific to work for and taught me a great deal about how to interact well with customers: never push, but encourage them and open their eyes to new possibilities. 'Remember, you don't buy a new dress because you need one,' Mary told me."

Judy Wolfinsohn Parker

"When you walked into the Gift Shop, you were immediately aware of design, and you had the feeling of something unusual. It was more like a gallery than a shop. Clothes were hanging on the wall above the glass, the pottery and wood were in the front, and up the steps, in the back, were the dress racks and two fitting rooms. The windows gave it light and air. It was quite remarkable."

Dorothy Dahl

"Mary was a wonderful teacher; she was enthusiastic. Mary always said she 'went looking for gold nuggets' on her buying trips. When she came back from her buying trips, she bubbled and told us where things came from and who made them."

Ilse Heyman

"My first days on the job were designed to help me master the skills of approaching and assisting customers. In addition I had to learn about the beautiful merchandise, so I could speak with some authority to the customers. My mentor and teacher who became my best friend for life was Ilse Heyman, who overlooked everything clumsy and slow about my early development and coached me into becoming a fairly poised salesperson."

Lucille Bell

"I had gone to Israel, and I brought wonderful jewelry from there. I worked with a woman in Israel who knew a great deal and traveled widely, and the jewelry that we sold was maybe the most beautiful jewelry that you could find. You don't find that any more. We sold it for much more than I paid. There were people [in Cambridge] who waited for the shipment. There was one woman who would buy practically everything that came in. I was very choosy, and my standards were tremendously high. Maybe for a business that's not always that good, but I couldn't have operated any other way.

"I think maybe the fascination of the Window Shop for me was partly that I was allowed to handle things my way, and that I could deal with people. I could never have worked for a commercial shop … it was a unique enterprise, really."

Mary Mohrer

"Profits for 1966 were unexpectedly high, $19K, this success due in part to the fortuitous weather and in part to Miss Mohrer's professional skill. She has kept salaries under control and has proved the Window Shop is a financially possible enterprise. In January, Gift Shop sales were up $2,500 over last year and the Restaurant $3,000. The buffet dinners have added to the Shop's success in general and helped to make January a wonderful month. Dinners were also up."

Board of directors meeting

"Usually at the end of the summer and the end of the winter certain things went on sale. Nowadays when you pay the full price for something, you feel cheated. When we had the sales, we had people who wore the Bardley suits—they were wonderful suits, and if they were on sale, you might take two.

"We had all kinds of ways, but most of all I think of the display of the merchandise, and Mary did that, pinning the dresses on that wall. Friday morning was display day, and let me tell you, it was hectic each Friday morning, because you had to do this and that, but in the end, the results were wonderful. And the first person who walked in, she wanted that dress that was up there. Of course you suggested, 'Try another size,' you did all kinds of things, and then if you could, you promised that when it came down, she would be called."

Tamar Wurmfeld

"Friday morning was display day, and it was hectic."

"Every Friday the glassware got washed, the clothes came down, we changed everything. We had a big showcase near the street so that people would know we were there because there was this long walkway. We changed that every second week. There was a very heavy board that we had to take in and out, and it was hard work, but we did it, and we had fun.

"Mary came back from a buying trip in July, and she had all sorts of ideas on how we would decorate the shop for Christmas. That was, of course, the big time, and we had squares in the ceiling, but porous, so you could stick pins in. And she had bought all these wonderful Christmas decorations made by Mr. Cheney on

Schroon Lake, and we would put long strings on them and pin them into the ceiling—and the whole Shop was lovely. It looked charming, but woe to the tall customer who would go and rip one out, and, 'No, no, don't do that, because we have to get up on the stepladder!'

"Another time she came back with the little lights on a string. Nobody used the little lights [before]. Mary threw them over the wisteria; she had them slung all over the windows."

Ilse Heyman

"All of us sold everything—casseroles, glassware, whatever we had. We had beautiful things. And then we had, for instance, customers who came for Christmas and sent gifts from the Window Shop to everybody. When we mailed, we had to write down the address, the sender—there were special books printed for that—the price, and so on, and from year to year, we had that for these special customers. We could pull them out, and we could say, 'Last year you sent this woman a casserole. I don't think you want to do that this year.' Or they would say, 'Could you tell me what I sent last year?' Which is a service, absolutely.

"And there was another thing for me—the gift wrapping. I came from Israel where you had to bring your bag if you want your rations. We gift wrapped, we put it in a box, we stuffed it with excelsior. I was still doing the packing for a number of years, until we hired people only for packing."

Tamar Wurmfeld

"Mary Halevy, who lived across the street, watched us and one day came to Mary [Mohrer] and said, 'Mary, I watch you two. I want to work with you.' She was born in Smyrna, Turkey, but grew up in Paris and had come here as a very young girl. Her husband also was Turkish, and after she had worked with us for a while she invited all of us, and there was this marvelous Oriental hospitality with all the Turkish goodies. She was wonderful; she was a live wire. She could sell you anything, and she could also sell you what you didn't want. She worked for us part-time, selling. She had learned dressmaking, she also could pin things and help with alterations, although I wasn't happy with the way she did alterations. But she sold more than anybody, but she was also the person whose merchandise often came back. When she saw people come in with boxes she knew she had sold them, she would say, 'Ilse, you're my lawyer! I don't want to have anything to do with it. You handle it!' So I had to. I liked Mary Halevy, even though we often were on opposite sides when it came to alterations."

Ilse Heyman

"During the holiday season, we were madly busy. When the days ended, we were so worn out that we were giddy with fatigue. One evening, in the winter darkness, the three of us—Mary, Ilse, and I—walked home through Harvard Square in a fresh flurry of snow. Suddenly I saw a $20 bill on the ground, not quite covered by the snow. We laughed and said it must have descended from heaven with the snow. I insisted that we share this unexpected gift. It was a lot of money in those days. But Mary and Ilse would have none of it. I arrived home quite a bit richer, my heart full of holiday mirth and affection for two generous and fun-loving women."

Lucille Bell

"When they renovated and made the bathroom downstairs from the Gift Shop, most people didn't see it because there was display here and a big wall there, and the door to the bathroom was there. [She gestures.] And a woman comes to me and asks me something. I couldn't understand what she wanted. She mumbled a bit, so I thought she wants the bathroom. People don't shout, 'Where's the bathroom?' They ask quietly, politely. So I sent her into the bathroom. Two seconds later she comes out, furious! Why did I send her in the bathroom? She wanted out!

"In the later years, groups of people came in, and all kinds of things happened. Clothes would disappear. I will never forget—Mary had bought some beautiful crystal eggs which were displayed quite in the front. And customers came in to the store, and customers came in to the counter, and one by one these eggs disappeared. I think from the dozen, we sold two. There was very little you could do.

"Then we had to count all the clothes every morning and every evening to find out if something happened. One time when Mary and Ilse went on a trip to buy, I was, so to speak, in charge, and there came in two people—a woman with a big handbag and a young man with her. They looked at suits—we had at that time knit suits. And in front of my eyes the knit suit disappeared. So I was after her, I confronted her, and in the meantime somebody called the police. You are not allowed to confront them until they leave the door, unless you see a tag running out or hanging out or something. I remember going out after them, which is something I know we shouldn't do, but I did because I wanted to stall them until the police came. Well, the police never came for half an hour. The way I stopped going after them is that he offered to knock my teeth in; she would not open her bag, and I knew that suit was in that bag. But, as a rule, you see, we were so spoiled with our customers we never had such problems."

Tamar Wurmfeld

"For a long time we had no cash register, just a wooden drawer. Mary said there was no space for a cash register, but our accountant, Fred Alexander, insisted that we had grown too large to keep the money in a drawer in the middle of the shop. So one day a monstrosity of a cash register was brought in. We created an area for it—a narrow corridor where we kept packing materials. Eventually we had a more modern cash register, but we never had one that did inventory."

Ilse Heyman

*Elsa Ulich, for whom the first Assistance
Fund was named.*

The Assistance Fund

"We voted to pay the camp expenses of about $50 for the eleven-year-old daughter of Mrs. K. of Brighton, Mass.," read a letter to the board president in August 1944. "Mrs. K. has been working in the Window Shop kitchen, is a very frail and nervous woman.... Her husband has left her, and the separation has badly affected the youngest child. Friends suggested that the child be sent to Mr. Moody's camp in Concord, N.H. In order to relieve her from this debt, we made the above decision."

Summer camp allowed Window Shop mothers to work more hours during the summer, and whenever possible, fees were paid from the Assistance Fund, one of the organization's signature successes. Over the years, hundreds of people—and not only those affiliated with the Window Shop—benefited from the Assistance Fund. Its original purpose was to help Window Shop employees and their families in "hardship situations," the needs ranging from English lessons to child care to very modest tuition costs for students. By today's standards, awards that ranged from $50 to $250 seem paltry indeed, but in the 1940s and 1950s, those amounts meant a great deal and were gratefully received.

The Assistance Fund began in January 1943, when Mrs. Arthur Koch brought her European hand-blocked linens to be sold at the shop. They sold for $149, and Mrs. Koch refused to take the proceeds, generously donating them to the shop.

Mary Mohrer suggested that the money be set aside as a training fund for Window Shop employees. In March 1944, the board voted to establish a broader Assistance Fund, supported by profits from the Restaurant and Gift and Dress Shop. The fund was inspired by then-President Elsa Brändström Ulich, and after her death in 1948 it was renamed the Ulich Fund in her memory. Annual solicitations to the Cambridge community augmented the shop's contributions, and the Ulich Fund was able to reach out to a wider population.

A member of the executive committee interviewed employees requesting financial assistance, and each month the committee voted on the awards to be granted. Some awards were loans, others were outright gifts. In 1944, its first full year of operation, scholarships ranging from $100 to $400 were awarded to ten people; four employees requested and received loans of $50 to $200 to help with medical expenses; and $81.30 covered the expenses of sending two Window Shop children to summer camp. Total gifts and loans that year came to $2,783. Figures reported for subsequent years were approximately the same, with a modest increase in numbers of people receiving assistance for tuition, medical expenses, and summer camp fees. Throughout the early 1940s, a few employees continued to request and receive assistance. In 1947 the Assistance Fund was suspended temporarily while the Window Shop moved to Brattle Street from Mount Auburn Street.

Ten years after it was begun, emphasis focused more exclusively on scholarship awards, and candidates were not necessarily connected with the Window Shop. In September 1952, among the loans awarded were $100 to an employee for violin lessons, $250 to an employee for career training as an x-ray technician, and $100 to a waitress for extra vacation pay because she was "emotionally fragile and needed a vacation badly." One of the shop's cooks, much loved by all, had a car accident and was unable to work for several weeks. The Assistance Fund paid the difference between the insurance company's coverage and her salary.

The 1954 Annual Report (dealing with the year 1953) by President Alice Cope expressed concern that the Window Shop's Retirement Plan "will cost considerable money," reducing the amount available for the Ulich Fund. She reported that of 115 people interviewed during the year for these funds, eighty-three had no connection with the Window Shop, and that tentative scholarships totaling approximately $2,000 were committed to seven students, three of whom were Window Shop children.

Fifteen years after the Ulich Fund was established, the Twentieth Anniversary [of the Window Shop] Report stated that "since 1948, $12,500 has been given for hardship situations and $46,000 for scholarship awards, as well as loans to employees or students. A total of 428 students have been helped by the Window Shop, either through part-time employment or scholarship grants from the Ulich

Fund.... The $46,000 was granted in 267 scholarship awards to 117 students. About 80 percent of them were from central Europe."

When the Window Shop closed in 1972, the board decided that the Ulich Fund should continue to aid foreign students and relatives of former Window Shop employees. The grants and loans would be financed with the income from the sale of the shop and from annual gift solicitations. The name was changed to the Window Shop, Inc. Scholarship Fund, and its activities from 1972 through 1987 are chronicled in Chapter 3.

Voices

"At the Window Shop Assistance Fund meeting, we voted to give to Mrs. O. of Brighton, Massachusetts, $200 to be paid out in three installments. Her husband, a Fuller Brush salesman, is in a full cast up to the heart because of an injury to his back. The physicians have not given him any certainty that this cure will help him, but they want to see the result after six weeks. If no result, they will consider an operation. Mrs. O. has had a stomach ulcer for years and is very often not able to work. Two boys are in training and cannot contribute for the moment to help their parents."

Letter to Elizabeth Aub from Elsa Brändström Ulich, Aug. 17, 1944

"I was born in Lwow, Poland, and in September 1939, fled with my family to Romania and then to Palestine. There, after finishing high school, I joined the Free Polish Forces and fought in Italy. After World War II ended, I studied engineering at the University of London. In 1949 I came to the U.S. as a displaced person and couldn't find a job. I had been admitted to MIT [Massachusetts Institute of Technology]. A kind man in New York loaned me some money to begin my studies, and I registered as a special student because my BSc [Bachelor of Science degree] results had not yet arrived from London. I was allowed to take graduate courses but was not eligible for a scholarship. Jewish Family Services in Boston could not assist me because I was not a Boston resident. A friend suggested I apply to the Window Shop, and I was given a critically important grant. Mrs. Alice Cope, who interviewed me, was also very welcoming and later invited me to dinners at her home. I became a part-time technician at RLE [Research Laboratory of Electronics] at MIT and was able to receive my MSEE degree. I later received a Ph.D. in applied physics from Harvard. When I finished my studies, I was delighted to be able to pay back my Window Shop grant."

Julian Bussgang

"A thirty-three-year-old Romanian lawyer, unmarried, could not hold a job. Jewish Vocational had to support him longer than any other émigré. In spite of negative comments from other agencies, we decided to support his attendance at summer school. He planned to acquire an M.A. in Sociology ... to become self-supporting. Based on his summer school marks, he was accepted in the Graduate Department of Sociology at B.U. [Boston University]. The Window Shop supported him through his first semester. In addition, we counseled him in the mores of American attitudes toward students and the importance of sticking out difficult room-and-board jobs in order to receive support from other community groups. Based on his outstanding grades, he was awarded an assistantship for the second semester and no longer needs Window Shop support.

"A twenty-two-year-old Greek émigré needs funds for an English language course."

Report by Deborah Hermann to executive committee, Feb. 16, 1967

"Several examples of people asking for/deserving of scholarship money—'young negro boy' on tuition scholarship at Shady Hill, English lessons for the wife of a grad student at MIT who was accepted at Brandeis on a scholarship with the understanding that she complete a college-level English course, college tuition for twin children of a Window Shop employee ...

"Mrs. Hermann brought up a recurring policy problem of the Ulich Fund: do we support students from other countries who will be returning home at the end of their training? In principle we would like to help them, but their financial needs are great and our resources small. We have confined such scholarships to those returning students who have been employed at the Window Shop and therefore are entitled to the same consideration as all employees with regard to scholarship aid."

Executive committee report, Feb. 28, 1967

"Within the last three years the Ulich Fund has added a new category of eligibility for scholarships—foreign students who intend to return to their homelands."

President's Report by Marion Bever, May 5, 1971

"I was a student at Harvard College, trying to make meager ends meet and to plan for graduate education. The situation seemed to be hopeless, and I was ready to quit when I walked into the Window Shop for my first interview. There was a warm, bright-eyed lady. I told her my woes and my intention to give up. She said, 'Oh, nonsense!' We had a long talk, and to my amazement cold cash and a rigid budget were hardly discussed. It was as though money was a secondary consideration, and when the need for it arose, it would be available. And it was! I walked out a new man with hopes."

Robert L. Berger, MD

"I came to this country in 1948, one of the many refugees who had lived through the war in German-occupied Poland.... Education was my only hope of making a place in this strange, new world. It was the Window Shop which made this hope a reality. I will always remember the interview at which I submitted the budget I needed to attend Radcliffe College. 'And what about a sum of joy?' This question characterizes the atmosphere in which help is given. Those seeking it are treated not as cases but as human beings. Here a *Displaced* person found her first *Place*.

Ilona Karmel Zucker

"Miss Edith Stedman [of Radcliffe College] had seen a Polish refugee [Ilona Karmel], at present in New York at Hunter College. She would like to transfer to Radcliffe. She is most attractive, has only one leg, but marvelous spirit. She needs a place to live near Radcliffe, $200 for support. [In March 1950, the student was awarded $101.]"

Executive committee minutes, Oct. 13, 1949

Social Services: Counseling, Referrals, and Friendship House

Mary Mohrer, manager of the Gift and Dress Shop, who was there from the beginning of the Window Shop, once said, "The Window Shop was a social agency without red tape." She herself was the "social worker" from the very beginning, helping refugees find a foothold in America, get jobs, secure housing, and learn English. "We always had a corner to meet in," she said. "There wasn't much office space, but there was a table and two chairs. And people would come at any time."

As the Window Shop grew more successful in the 1940s, especially after its move to Brattle Street, the employee base grew as well. So did the profits, which were turned over to the new Assistance Fund. Now the workers could have money readily available to them quickly and without red tape, either on loan or as an outright grant when an emergency arose, and scholarship money would be available to them or their children.

The Window Shop was a nonprofit organization, whose purpose was to provide jobs and be self-supporting, with profits going into the Assistance Fund. With financial success in the late 1940s came the evolutionary policy of hiring as many part-time workers as possible. Whoever needed work was offered a job in the kitchen or as a waitress for a short time until she could find more suitable employment elsewhere. Although a nucleus of permanent employees provided continuity, training and support to the newcomers, the board came to realize that "employment should be given to those in need, on the basis of their need rather than on the basis of their training or skill or ability."[25] Broadly speaking, this meant that the Window Shop often employed people who were, strictly speaking, either unqualified or overqualified for the job. Alice Cope cited the example of the seventy-year-old former German judge who, basically unemployable in the legal profession in the United States, typed and mimeographed the menus each day. A majority of the women had not worked outside the home before. "We give employment to the physically handicapped, [to] students who can work only a few hours a day, and to some women who can work only a few hours per week," said Mrs. Cope. "The only requirement is that they understand the spirit of the Shop and join in it."[26]

This paradigm of employment would not be possible in the contemporary business world with its emphasis exclusively on the "bottom line." The shop's success in financial and human terms attests to the indomitable spirit of the employees and the board members, working together to create a unique enterprise.

The refugees who arrived at the Window Shop after World War II were mostly "Displaced Persons," many beset by mental and physical ills. Having survived long years of hardship and privation, their struggle to make sense of their new world must have seemed insurmountable. The Window Shop found ways to help. As Alice Cope said, "We did not wish to become a social agency, and we did not wish to provide casework service. We have, therefore, never employed a professional social worker, and all the work of advising has been done by volunteers."

People with medical needs and personal problems were referred to social agencies in the community, but often a helping hand stretched out from employee to employee was all that was needed. One employee helped a newcomer find an apartment in her building, board members sponsored hundreds of refugees seeking citizenship, and workers and board members alike opened their homes or loaned furniture to the refugee newly arrived, exhausted, bewildered, and in need of a job. Stories of young refugees sheltering with board members for a year or longer were not uncommon.

In her interviews in the mid-1980s, Mary Mohrer told of her many experiences in counseling refugee families at all hours of the day or night. After all, she was their peer—a fellow refugee who had blazed a trail for them. She remembered a refugee "who was really close to suicide. I sat with her, and I just wouldn't have dared to go home and leave her. She had married a GI and come to this country. She had a Ph.D.; he came from a small New England town and was apparently not at all educated. She was not Jewish, but she came into a family of Irish Catholics who were churchgoing. Her husband didn't want her to work, but he didn't give her any money either. She didn't even have the money to take a streetcar. She had to go to church not only on Sunday, but every day to Mass. She couldn't go home because there was no money. She was at the end of it all. I called Mrs. Ulich and told her I didn't dare leave. She said they had dinner guests, but she would come as soon as she could. She came toward midnight, and she helped this woman to go back home."[27]

Voices

"The postwar refugees suffering from illness, and there were many, were referred to hospitals and their social service departments, to individual doctors and dentists, and to social agencies whose professional counseling skills were invaluable. The Window Shop's volunteers became expert in housing, educational possibilities, and job-finding, said Alice Cope.[28] In addition, they met the boats that brought Displaced Persons to Boston after the war. On weekends I went to the harbor to help newly arrived people. I carried luggage and sorted luggage with [social workers]. I talked with them because I spoke their language. I later very often saw them at the Window Shop, but at the harbor I actually did the dirty work. The social workers from the refugee committees did the rest, and they did a very good job.

"Over the years we helped hundreds of people. When you think of families, [think of] women who married GIs and were stranded, people who really wanted a divorce and didn't know where to go, women who got pregnant and didn't know what to do. The problems that were handled were manifold."

Mary Mohrer

"Gradually, the Window Shop ... became a referral center for jobs, housing, English lessons, help in readjusting to this strange new country, medical care, education, and a myriad of other problems which faced the newcomers. Its volunteers became experts in all the available sources of help. Perhaps the most important help was just being there to show concern, to answer questions, to reassure ...

"The newcomers seemed prone to more illness than the average person. It was supposed this was due to the tremendous emotional and financial strains they had been through and also lack of medical care during the early years in the United States. So developed a whole network of referrals to hospitals and their social service departments, to individual doctors and dentists, to social agencies."

Alice Cope

Friendship House

Frances Fremont-Smith was one of the visionary board members whose chief contribution to the Window Shop touched the early refugees in tangible and enduring ways. Friendship House was her idea—a meeting place for employees to gather socially with Americans from the Cambridge community. In January 1943, Friendship House opened in the Window Shop's lunchroom (at 102 Mount Auburn Street), which was not used in the evening. The board contributed $500 toward expenses, and Mrs. Fremont-Smith organized events.

Harvard professors gave lectures on Monday evening. "Young Arthur Schlesinger [Jr.] talked to an interested group about Jacksonian Democracy before his book was published," reported Marion Muller in her 1959 history of the shop. "One evening Professor Howard Mumford Jones stood before the earnest group, pulled a dollar bill from his pocket, and said, 'I want to show you a picture,' and talked about George Washington and America."

A lending library was set up, English lessons were offered (and enthusiastically received), and social times were held on some weekends. In a 1985 interview, Mrs. Fremont-Smith said, "It was very attractive. People could stay and have a game of bridge or whatever. A great deal of telephoning and persuading had to be done to be sure that there were hostesses and men from the community. I know of several cases where firm friendships were made at Friendship House." She pointed out that there were quite a number of single men among the refugees who were accustomed to going to cafés in their home countries to read the newspaper and talk with other men. "These men were very lonely," said Mrs. Fremont-Smith. "We just don't do that in our restaurants in this country. This part of Friendship House was very helpful to those men, [especially those] who did not have large families or contacts." About the English lessons, Mrs. Fremont-Smith observed, "The refugees were all very intent on learning English. They had to. Many of them were very well educated, and these contacts at Friendship House had a lot to do with perfecting their English."

Friendship House closed in the spring of 1944, perhaps due to a combination of bad weather and the successful assimilation of the refugees into the community. The lectures and English lessons continued for some time after the closing. Despite its short life, Friendship House provided a much-needed, fast-track introduction to the American way of life for the newest immigrants to these shores.

Voices

"The purpose [of Friendship House] was for these people, coming out of Nazi Germany and Austria, to be able to meet Americans who would both become their friends and be very helpful to them in many matters besides money and profession. Questions about the children, where to live, where to market, and so forth … all those little details.… The most difficult part was to find Cantabrigians to come Sunday afternoon to meet them.…

"We paid for a Cambridge woman who liked the idea of earning a little money and of being the hostess. She could serve tea and coffee; there were tables and comfortable chairs."

Frances Fremont-Smith

"It was important at the beginning to have a social connection with the refugees, where they could talk and improve their English and knowledge of American ways. Perhaps after the early, frantic times passed, it was harder for people living in Cambridge to give their Sunday afternoons, and possibly as the newcomers became used to their new surroundings, the organized meetings became less important to them as well."

Dorothy Dahl

"One elderly American lady, having sat over a cup of tea with a group of new-comers her own age, said on leaving, 'They are a remarkable group. I would never be able to manage if the same thing happened to me.'"

Alice Cope

"With integration of refugees in the social life of the community, its [Friendship House's] need no longer seems great. There will be lectures this month arranged by Mrs. Henderson and Mrs. Schlesinger, plus four Sunday afternoons when Army officers studying German may meet and talk German with groups of refugees."

Board of directors meeting, Nov. 16, 1943

Board President Elizabeth Aub and staff member Martha Washington.

Personnel Policies and Benefits

The Window Shop was a progressive organization for its time, not only because of its mission, its services, and its policy of hiring (and accommodating) as many employees as possible, but also because of its liberal personnel practices.

In March 1942, the board established the Committee on Personnel Practices, with Bernice Cannon as chair. Under Miss Cannon's expert leadership, the committee spent an astounding five years analyzing the Window Shop in regard to employment: hours of work, wages, vacations, holidays, and other issues. This must have been a very thorough process, since Marion Muller's history of the Window Shop describes "a patient, careful project, reading records and even searching memories before records began, conferring with managers, the treasurer, and other managers."[29]

In 1943, accident and sickness insurance (with Blue Cross/Blue Shield) was made available to all employees, and workmen's compensation became federal law for nonprofits. The personnel committee's recommendations on key policies were made and voted on by the board of directors in the late 1940s and were printed in pamphlet form for employees and managers.

In the fall of 1950, Social Security was extended to nonprofits, much to the relief of the older Window Shop employees. Moreover, the board was considering a pension plan to supplement Social Security; that plan took effect in August 1954.

Mrs. Muller reported that the employees' health problems were of great concern to the managers, and the Committee on Personnel Practices recommended extended coverage for illness insurance. In addition, the committee recommended that the hours of work for employees aged fifty-five and older be reduced, but their salaries remain the same. The shop paid for annual physical examinations by the Window Shop physician, Dr. Robert Buka, for all employees who wanted them, and all workers were required to have a medical exam before being hired.

In the mid-1950s, the Window Shop was very successful, and the profits resulted in substantial contributions to the pension fund, the group life insurance program, the extension of the health plan, and to the sickness and accident insurance coverage. As the Window Shop grew and prospered, its employment policies became more established. The board of directors formalized the policy of employing more people than were needed, both part-time and full-time, to give jobs to as many refugees as possible. Another policy was to hire some American-born workers who would work side-by-side with the newcomers, each learning from the other. As part of this group, several African Americans (then called Negroes) were hired; allegedly, the Window Shop was the first shop in Cambridge to employ blacks. With success, too, came modestly higher wages.

One of the jewels in the Window Shop's crown was the Assistance Fund, later called the Ulich Fund, and finally the Scholarship Fund. It is described more fully in Chapters 2 and 3. It stands as a paradigm of employee assistance and scholarship aid that is undoubtedly unrivaled by any other organization of its time.

Voices

"When Miss Cannon retired, she still remained on the committee from sheer interest, and because she was urged. Two people were chosen as cochairmen. In their first report, they wrote, 'It soon became apparent that the rather spasmodic and inaccurate fire of two popguns could never equal the value and power of a long-range Cannon.'"

Marion Muller

"With increased financial security, there has been more time to look at the needs of the people involved. The reduced efficiency of the older group has added to the already heavy pressure put on those responsible for running the Restaurant in particular. Getting and giving supplementary help without undermining the position of the older workers adds to both the cost and the fatigue.

"We have required a medical checkup by the Window Shop doctor for all employees over sixty-five. This compulsory examination, unlike the voluntary annual one we offer, is made with the clear understanding that the doctor will recommend to the Executive Committee any change in hours or position which he considers advisable in the interest of the employee's health."

Elizabeth Aub, President's Report, 1963

"For the comparatively small group of the elderly or handicapped, the Window Shop has become a 'holding corporation'—something not in the original plan but actually an accepted policy from the time we instituted a Pension Plan. For this group of about ten people, the Shop has been everything—employer, family, and friend. The various benefits of insurances, medical care, Pension Plan, etc., have taken the place, to some extent, of the savings they would have had had they not been uprooted and sent penniless to this land. It would be unthinkable to do other than keep these people going as well and as long as possible no matter what the burden to others of the cost of about six supplementary helpers required."

Elizabeth Aub, President's Report, 1962

"We have had for some time a young woman in our bakery who, like her husband, comes from a Nazi background in Germany. She was taken on with some feelings of trepidation. Now she is on excellent terms with everyone and is developing into a superior person. Another baker, an elderly Frenchman, charmed his way into our kitchen before we knew of his strong anti-Semitic feelings. Before long his whole attitude changed. Last summer, at the request of Christ Church, we took in a young Mohammedan Egyptian student. He worked side by side with young Israelis and all the others. When he left, he kissed everyone good-bye. We have Negroes throughout the Restaurant and not all in menial positions by any means. In close contact with them are Dutch Indonesian refugees who never knew such a relationship before. To create an atmosphere which can absorb happy individuals with such varied backgrounds and early prejudices is no mean achievement. If we did nothing else, this would seem to me to justify our existence."

Elizabeth Aub, President's Report, 1963

"The peak of our profits was not last year [1964], but in the years '57, '60, and '61. Since that time, the net profit for the year has declined markedly. The Sunday closing of the Restaurant in winter accounts for much of this. Higher rates for Blue Cross, Social Security, etc., have increased our expenses. But the largest increase in cost is in the payroll. Carrying our older workers accounts for some of this, but most of it is due to raising salaries, thereby making them equivalent to what the job commands elsewhere."

Elizabeth Aub, President's Report, 1965

"[New Restaurant Manager Guy Greco] has tried to upgrade some long-term workers instead of replacing them with more efficient, new workers. He also pressed the board to apply for unemployment insurance, which has only recently become available to nonprofit institutions, and to increase the employer's share of Blue Cross payments."

Marion Bever, President's Report, 1971

Eleanor Roosevelt (right) meets three women from the Bakery.

The Customers Have Their Say

The Window Shop's customers were the third leg of a three-legged stool; the board and the employees were the other two essential components. None could function without the others.

In the beginning, the customers were Europeans who went to the Window Shop Tea Room and Bakery to taste familiar food. At its twentieth anniversary, Board Member Marion Muller wrote of the Cambridge community, "The Shop, with its European atmosphere, food, clothes, gifts, and foreign accents, has been cordially accepted."[30]

"People in Cambridge had a proprietary feeling about the Window Shop," said former Board President Dorothy Dahl.

As its reputation spread, the Window Shop's customer base expanded to include not only local professors, students, their parents, and Cambridge residents, but celebrities, who made it their destination when they visited Cambridge. Eleanor Roosevelt and Henry Kissinger were perhaps two of the best-known repeat customers, but former employees also tell of visits to the Restaurant and Gift Shop by film stars Elizabeth Taylor, Hume Cronyn, and Jessica Tandy. Celebrities ordered their wedding cakes from the Bakery, and Swissair was a regular customer for pastries (undoubtedly for its first-class passengers!).

The Christmas season brought a variety of customers to the Window Shop for unique gifts and for special baked goods for holiday parties. The relationship between the employees and the customers was just as unique as everything else about the Window Shop. Staff and customers became friends, Gift and Dress Shop employees would alert their best customers to incoming merchandise, and board members brought their well-heeled friends to shop and dine there.

An anecdote is told by a well-known Cambridge businessman, who dined at the famous Hotel Sacher in Vienna. After a superb meal, he ordered *Sacher torte* for dessert. "Oh, sir," replied the waiter. "I don't recommend the *Sacher torte*. The only place in the world you can get a good *Sacher torte* is at the Window Shop in Cambridge, Massachusetts."

Thirty-three years after the Window Shop closed, former customers still remember it fondly and miss its distinct and comfortable presence on Brattle Street.

Toward the end, the Window Shop board decided not to tell the employees of the impending demise of the shop, fearing that the customers would find out. In retrospect, this was an unwise decision: it seems obvious that the affluent and influential customer base would have rallied in defense of the Window Shop, perhaps extending its life for several more years and surely making its eventual demise far less painful for everyone than it was.

Voices

"My first memories [of the Window Shop] are of the Restaurant in the very late forties and early fifties. It was the perfect venue for dinner with one's parents while we were in college. I distinctly remember two wonderful dishes: the duck with candied fruit and the outstanding *Sauerbraten*....

"The desserts, of course, were marvelous, both at the Restaurant and when ordered to take home. Cookies galore, *Linzer torte,* and my favorites, the *petits fours*. I always ordered a large fondant tree for Christmas or a bell for New Year's Eve, and the *Bûche de Noel* was a real treat with its meringue mushrooms.

"One day my husband phoned to say he was bringing a Russian scientist home for dinner. I either bought or made the Window Shop borscht, a lovely cold soup—pink, with sour cream. The visitor said it was excellent, but would I tell him what it was! It was not, of course, the heavy Russian cabbage soup, and I learned not to try to please foreign visitors with food of their own countries.

"We learned so much about Viennese food, which was not only delicious, but also connected us to a Europe of the past, and that connection was epitomized by the staff. The Window Shop was a magnet for academic émigrés, Viennese psychoanalysts, Cambridge Brahmins, and us young Americans who were being introduced to the culture of prewar Europe. Entertaining was so much easier when we could bring home goodies, sure that they would please. I once asked how many servings a certain cake would allow. The answer was, 'Eight, but Mrs. Wyzanski gets thirteen.'"

Ann Karnovsky

"In the Gift Shop we had a very, very faithful clientele. As a salesperson, I had tried to tell a customer, 'I don't think that's for you,' because, as Mary said, 'I don't want her to walk out with a dress and have everybody say to her, "Who in heaven's name sold you this dress?"' On the other hand, we had some brands at the time, it was called Petite Four (most people thought it was something to eat), it was for shorter people and not necessarily a woman's figure. So when I had a customer and she fitted in those well, I could call up and say, 'We got a new shipment in. If you have any interest, come on in.' That doesn't mean I forced her to come in. But they were eternally grateful; if you are hard to fit, and you have a salesperson who knows what you want, oh, you are so grateful!"

Tamar Wurmfeld

"I remember some dresses that I bought, and I'm sure that Miss Heyman or Mary Mohrer helped me. I remember a fussy green dress with a bow that was my first sort of dressy dress, and it was made for someone at least twenty years older than me! It was quite inappropriate, and when my cousin was married in 1952, I bought a dress, which I still own because I loved it so much. I still have it upstairs—I couldn't get into it now for anything, but it had a scoop neck, big puffy sleeves, green and white stripes, damasky kind of silk, with a big skirt, tight-fitting bodice. Beautifully made; I loved that dress.

"Everything we bought came from the Window Shop. One year, around 1946 or '47, I had earned enough money to buy my parents a set of old-fashioned glasses; they drank old-fashioneds always. They had little birds on them, and we still have a couple of them.

"We often ate at the Restaurant. I remember borscht and Viennese salad, and I remember *Linzer torte*. It seems to me my mother [Elizabeth Aub] ate there several times a week, and I might have eaten there several times a month. That's when my sister Franny was waiting on tables, and Mary Churchill, her friend from next door, also worked there."

Nancy Aub Gleason

"The Window Shop became very much of a family institution. My mother took friends there to eat and also bought desserts to take home. I wasn't that keen on Viennese food; I found it too rich, and I rarely ate there unless I was taken in specifically. I liked the fact that they carried Lanz clothes. They had a wonderful range of imports that I liked. I remember buying a gorgeous Icelandic sweater there and also an Icelandic coat, sort of a long jacket, probably in the late '60s or early '70s. I think I bought more clothes there than anyplace else. Nobody bugged you—'what would you like?' and so on. I could take my time over it."

Ruth Hubbard Wald

"Dirndls, authentic Lanz-made ones, were woven into all the pleasures of the Window Shop. I was sorry when I got too old for them. It seems so sort of quaint now and such a simple pleasure, but it really was great to go to the Window Shop for supper. Was there something special about Wednesday night supper? Bobby [Cope, her brother] always ordered *Wiener Schnitzel* with an egg on top. He also loved *Linzer torte*. I wondered how he learned about things like that."

Eliza Cope Harrison

"By the time the Window Shop moved to 56 Brattle Street in 1947, it had become a favorite haunt for the diverse community of European intellectuals who fled to Cambridge, such as architect Walter Gropius. The Continental food and atmosphere provided a welcome link to their past. 'It makes people feel at home to find here in Cambridge goodies they had … in their childhood,' Alice Broch told the *Christian Science Monitor* in 1955."

The Boston Globe, Jan. 4, 1995

"There was a couple, the Kaplans, who routinely appeared from New Hampshire on the last Saturday of the Christmas season to buy gifts for their employees, usually around 4:00 or even 5:00 PM. Mrs. Kaplan sat down at a table in the Restaurant with all her cards and mailing labels and ordered coffee and pastry, while her husband walked through the Shop taking from the shelves whatever appealed to him and taking them to his wife for approval. The Kaplans owned a textile mill in New Hampshire and gave their employees very generous gifts. Within minutes, the Shop was denuded, and Tamar [Wurmfeld] and I ran back and forth replacing the items. Meanwhile, it was almost closing time, which did not disturb the Kaplans. Eventually, they were done. We were all ready to collapse, but after we rang up the total, we said, 'Hallelujah!' On Monday we would pack up and ship the order."

Ilse Heyman

"About a week before Christmas, Mrs. Broch would say to me, 'Now, Pearl, no more orders for Yule logs or *Linzer tortes* for Christmas.' But my customers (and I was on a first-name basis with all my customers) without fail would call me up at the last minute and order something like five *Linzer tortes*. I'd say, 'Why are you calling now?' I was able to speak to them like that because they knew me. They would say, 'Pearl, I have to have …' I would go to Doris [the head baker], and she would sneak a few more in. I'd go home at the end of the day, and I was, like, crazy because I didn't want to let my customers down, and at the same time I felt bad for Doris."

Pearl Morrison

"I shall never be at a loss where to take one of my grandchildren for a delightful meal if I find myself in Cambridge…. So many happy faces greeted me there—these women who had been in concentration camps or had spent long years waiting to find themselves able to begin life again in a new country, and now actually at work helping their husbands or their children to start again. You are glad you live in an America which can be a land of hope."

Eleanor Roosevelt, "My Day," May 30, 1950

"My mother [Sally Wolfinsohn] and I were at the Shop the day Mrs. Roosevelt visited. Mom was partially in charge. We all ate lunch with her, were introduced, and helped her choose gifts for her family. Snapshots of that day remain fixed in my mind. Mrs. Roosevelt was the idol of my generation (I was about seventeen at the time) and the idol of my mother's generation as well. It took months for the thrill to fade. Maybe it never quite did."

Judy Wolfinsohn Parker

"I'll never forget when Mrs. Roosevelt and Mr. [Henry] Morgenthau [III] came for lunch, and everybody got excited. After lunch she came out into the Gift Shop. Everybody kind of stood back, respectful. Finally, I approached her and said, 'May I help you?' 'Yes,' she said, 'I would like a Christmas gift for my granddaughter.' And we chose a few things. At the same time, being Mrs. Roosevelt, she asked where I came from, what I did, and so on. Then she wanted the gifts shipped out, and then she said, 'Could I charge them?' 'Of course you can charge them,' I said. I didn't have the authority to say that, but I did! That woman was just great! That day was one of my highlights."

Tamar Wurmfeld

"We all proceeded to The Window Shop on Brattle Street, which I remembered visiting many years ago, and where I had had such a good meal that I thought even our two gentlemen (Henry Kissinger and Henry Morgenthau III) would enjoy luncheon."

Eleanor Roosevelt, "My Day," date and year are unidentified

"The Window Shop was always for both of us a kind of home. How often did Felix refuse invitations to go out for dinner in a fancy place, saying simply, 'I do not like restaurants. Let's go to the Window Shop!'"

Dr. Helene Deutsch

"This is a place where even waitresses read Rainer Maria Rilke, and where almost everybody speaks with an accent."

Anonymous customer

"Our customers were an interesting mix of Brattle Street ladies for lunch, displaced European professors who confused us with the European coffeehouse and expected us to know what they wanted to eat without lifting their head from their newspaper, and Harvard and MIT students with their dates and visiting parents from all over the country."

Nadia Ehrlich Finkelstein

Mary Mohrer reads a tribute to Alice Broch (seated at table) at the farewell party for Mrs. Broch.

Three

The Winds of Change

Immediately following World War II, refugees who had survived Hitler came to the United States from European Displaced Persons camps. By the end of the 1940s, a different Europe had emerged, mostly due to the aggressive tactics of the USSR, which had been a central ally in defeating Germany. Now people emigrated to the United States from Europe as political refugees and were welcomed exuberantly as "freedom fighters" resisting Communism. These refugees differed from the mostly Jewish immigrants who had come before.

Hungarians, who came in this first wave, reflected these changes. They were mostly young, ambitious, charming, often artistic, delighted to be so welcomed—but had little interest in the bakery or restaurant work available at the Window Shop. A President's Report in 1964[31] states, "When the wave of Hungarian refugees arrived, the Window Shop expected to be swamped with applications for jobs. We weren't. The few who tried it found the work too hard or the hours too early or late, so that only one or two stuck it out long enough to learn either the job or the language." The Ulich Fund helped many of these newcomers with their educational expenses, but the board saw no other way to generate interest in the new immigrants. It was difficult to feel related to them; these newcomers had a fairly clear idea of what they would like to do and found support from several Hungarian relief organizations that helped them do it.[32]

In 1959, the Window Shop celebrated its twentieth anniversary. For the occasion, a study was made of the countries of origin of its employees and, separately, of those who had received welfare or educational assistance from the Ulich Fund. Employees were divided into four groups: those with fifteen to twenty years of service, those with ten to fifteen years, those with five to ten years, and those who had been Window Shop employees for less than five years.

In the oldest group, with fifteen to twenty years of service, 90 percent were German or Austrian, and 10 percent were American-born. In the group with ten to fifteen years at the shop, the ratio dropped to 65 percent German- or Austrian-born to 35 percent Americans. In the next group of employees with five to ten years of service, 44 percent were from Germany or Austria, and 31 percent were from the United States, with the remaining 25 percent from other parts of Europe. Of those with five years or less as employees, only 4 percent were German or Austrian, and 47 percent were American, with the remaining 49 percent from other European countries. In twenty years' time, the ratio of Germans/Austrians had shifted from 90 percent to only 4 percent, compared with 10 percent Americans to 47 percent—a sea change in the employee demographics.

Similarly, of the group that received family or educational help from the Ulich Assistance Fund in this twenty-year study, 80 percent were from Europe, including not only Germany and Austria, but Poland, Yugoslavia, Hungary, Czechoslovakia, France, Switzerland, and Northern Europe. The other 20 percent in this mostly student group were from the Near East, Asia, South America, and the United States.[33]

Also in the 1950s, the Window Shop hired its first African American employees. Alice Cope, former board president, asserts that, "The Window Shop was the first restaurant to hire blacks." Notable among the early African Americans was short-order cook Martha Washington, warm and motherly, who was a favorite among staff and customers alike. Most Europeans were unfamiliar with African Americans, but true to the Window Shop's atmosphere of tolerance and acceptance, blacks and whites worked side by side without conflict, and eventually, with mutual respect.

The winds of change drifted into Harvard Square in the fifties and picked up speed in the sixties. Some changes affecting the Window Shop were less obvious than the global geopolitical shifts that had brought new immigrants. When the

Window Shop moved to Brattle Street in 1947, it was unique; the Restaurant, Bakery, and Gift and Dress Shop sold goods not readily available elsewhere. By the mid-fifties, boutiques offering good design and restaurants serving European fare appeared in Harvard Square, competing with the Window Shop. Furthermore, while the Window Shop Restaurant had secured a wine and beer license in 1954, it could not serve liquor, which made fully licensed local restaurants more attractive to diners who enjoyed a martini before dinner.

The Harvard Square environment changed more drastically in the sixties. The Vietnam War was especially traumatic for area students and faculty. Their frustration and anger escalated to war protests, and there were nights in Harvard Square when dinner customers were not comfortable walking to their cars, parked farther and farther away as spaces were increasingly hard to find. Some locals considered the Square "unsafe," which was disquieting to residents who thought of Cambridge as a comfortable and intellectually stimulating "village." As a result, fewer Window Shop dinners were served, leaving managers and board members uneasy and uncertain as to what, if anything, they could do about it.

The limitations of the physical plant began to irritate everyone: the impossibly small kitchen, the need to transport food to the second-floor dining rooms by dumbwaiter, and the layout of the dining rooms, which made dinners seem more crowded than lunches (the pejorative "tea room" was occasionally heard from customers, which sounded demeaning to the employees and managers).

Outside in the garden, customers enjoyed lunches and dinners in good weather. An oasis in Cambridge, the garden at the Blacksmith House remained beautiful, exciting, and imaginatively lit by small white lights on the ancient wisteria vines on the old house. The Window Shop was a magnet, but only in good weather. Profits for the Restaurant were always tied to the weather, and the New England weather continued its fickle ways. Soon other restaurants discovered the popularity of outdoor dining, first introduced on Brattle Street.

A "marked decline" in profits was noted for 1963, compared with previously profitable years of 1957, 1960, and 1961. Contributing to the Window Shop's bleak economic picture were higher expenses (Blue Cross, Social Security), the Sunday closing of the Restaurant in the winter, and especially the increased payroll. Salaries had been raised throughout the organization, making them equivalent to others in the area.

It was at this juncture, in October 1963, that the beloved Alice Broch, longtime manager of the Restaurant and quite simply its heart and soul, announced her departure at the end of the year because of her husband's illness. Since 1942 she had taken courses in culinary arts and restaurant management, read the literature, and learned bookkeeping, and she knew instinctively about respecting, managing, and loving people. She made peace when necessary and never forgot to thank each board member and employee for tasks, no matter how small, done for the shop. In return, Alice Broch earned the affection of the entire Window Shop family.

Mrs. Broch's departure in December 1963 precipitated a crisis that the Window Shop was, surprisingly, unprepared to handle and from which it would never fully recover. "Nothing less than the future of the Window Shop was at stake when we lost Mrs. Broch," said Board President Elizabeth Aub, "not only as manager of our Restaurant but also as leader of the large and varied groups of people out of which she made a team of devoted assistants."[34] The otherwise estimable Mrs. Broch had not trained a successor, and her two next-in-command officers, Lotte Benfey and Elisabeth Martens, had declined the board's offer to be co-managers.

The board's response was to hire a new manager, Lotte Eisenberg, a native German who had immigrated to Israel. She was "discovered" by two traveling board members in Tiberias, Israel, where Miss Eisenberg managed an inn. They recommended that the board hire her to replace Mrs. Broch, which they did with enthusiasm. Miss Eisenberg was to arrive in Cambridge in March 1964, but months before her arrival, she requested renovations to the kitchen costing an estimated $50,000. "The amount is staggering," sputtered one board member. She also asked for increased salaries for the managers and proper offices for herself, Mrs. Benfey, and Mrs. Martens. The board agreed to these changes, but deferred the kitchen renovation for a year. A new office was built above the Gift Shop, with a stairway to the kitchen. (Only Mrs. Broch could have thought of her two square feet of space and a stool in a noisy kitchen as an "office" for the manager, commented a board president.)

Once she arrived to occupy her new office, Miss Eisenberg displayed intelligence, energy, and new ideas. Some of her innovations were inappropriate—for example, she changed the décor of the upstairs dining rooms to a colonial style that she felt would be more appropriate to the historic house, but it was totally incompatible with the Window Shop culture. Her other ideas addressed fundamental problems, however, and some were sound and to the point. In a report to the board of directors on October 26, 1964, Miss Eisenberg stressed the importance of profit-making to support the Ulich Fund. To maximize profits, she recommended appealing to new, younger customers through advertising; providing professional food service training for Restaurant employees; and keeping the Window Shop plant properly maintained through repairs and replacement when needed. "We must keep the place looking good," she insisted.

At that same meeting, the board discussed—yet again—where the Window Shop was headed. Board Member Walter Bieringer, a devoted friend to refugee causes and an experienced businessman, asked an unpopular question: how many unemployable people were employed and was it worth keeping the shop going for them? Considerable discussion ensued, and the board agreed that, "We still serve a valuable and useful purpose in the community; we should attempt to extend our communication with social agencies; we're doing a valuable job with our elderly employees and Negroes." It concluded by recommending that a subcommittee study long-range policies.[35]

Two days later, Mr. Bieringer wrote the following letter to Board President Alice Cope, which would be prophetic:

> It seems now that the vast majority of Board Members are willing to spend a huge sum [$50K for kitchen renovations] without knowing the present situation accurately, and without knowing where we will be in five or ten years from now. There may not be many refugees coming during the next five or ten years. This is something one cannot foretell.
>
> I suppose it is worthwhile keeping the Window Shop just for people who can't be employed elsewhere, but I couldn't even get an answer to that one—namely, how many such people did we have there at the present time.
>
> No Board ever wants to give up an organization when a job has been finished and few Boards are willing to change their operations for new purposes. In this case our Board is so emotional about the Window Shop that nothing can be wrong and asking well-intentioned questions seems to be insulting.[36]

Despite her professional expertise and talent, Lotte Eisenberg's personality was incompatible with the Restaurant staff, who still grieved the loss of their leader, Mrs. Broch. They complained bitterly to the board about Miss Eisenberg's shortcomings. In truth, she had arrived at a time of drastic change and uncertainty, and her tenure was undoubtedly doomed, following on the heels of the seemingly irreplaceable Alice Broch. Furthermore, she did not understand the history and culture of the Window Shop. She resigned in February 1965 and returned to Israel.

Once again the Restaurant was left without a capable manager. In late 1965 longtime board member Frank Vorenberg, the owner of Gilchrist's Department Store in Boston, suggested that the board use the proven expertise at hand and ask Mary Mohrer, manager extraordinaire of the Gift and Dress Shop, to become the general manager of the entire Window Shop. It was she who, as the Window Shop's first employee, had transformed a one-room consignment shop into the incomparable Gift and Dress Shop. Along the way she learned bookkeeping, trained her employees, and offered high-quality, innovative merchandise guaranteed to appeal to her ever-growing customer base. Her shop had always made a profit, and it was this profit that continually supported the rocky Restaurant and Bakery. But she had never managed a restaurant.

Mary Mohrer was reluctant to take on this challenge, understanding much better than the board (or anyone else in the organization) how difficult this would be. Although she had no restaurant experience, she was aware of the internecine warfare that often erupts in that stressful atmosphere. But she knew that her assistant, Ilse Heyman, could assume greater responsibilities in the Gift Shop, and she could rely on the experience of long-term Restaurant supervisors, Mrs. Benfey and Mrs. Martens, who would be her assistants. Mary's loyalty to the Window Shop finally overcame her misgivings, and in March 1965, she took the new job with energy and optimism. Within eighteen months, however, Mrs. Martens and Mrs. Benfey had retired, and the fortunes of the Window Shop began a slow downward spiral.

The Window Shop courtyard. The Gift Shop is at the rear of the courtyard.

Demise of a Cambridge Institution

When Mary Mohrer became general manager of the Window Shop, she soon improved the appearance of the dining room by applying the good taste and exceptional sense of style that were the hallmarks of her Gift Shop. Although the operation of the Gift Shop was stable under Assistant Manager Ilse Heyman, the Restaurant was still beset with a vast and disheartening array of problems that included charges of stealing by a kitchen worker, "bullying" of the kitchen staff by the cook, and carelessness by Bakery staff at the counter where products were sold ("a certain laxness in handling food … has been noticed. A piece of waxed paper must be used whenever food is to be moved or sold…."[37]).

Mary did her best to improve conditions in dining room service: "Each waitress will have a block of new paper for taking customers' orders rather than the old, torn-up, discarded menus they have been using," she ordered. "Butter on ice is to be served with a fork from a glass bowl at dinner time."[38] In addition to upgrading the amenities, she focused on increased efficiency and productivity in the kitchen and dining rooms, working intensively with the staff.

The year 1965 was promising, and customers remarked on the new décor. Christmas, always a holiday cherished by the staff, the customers, and the board, because the decorations and the food often brought lump-in-the-throat memories of times gone by, was successful. Some customers simply brought their holiday and Christmas lists to the Window Shop to be filled, gift-wrapped, and mailed, knowing that the selections would be perfect.

After a strong December 1965 profits report, sales in both the Restaurant and Gift Shop were "poor" by the end of January 1966. The board was compelled to begin discussing the future direction of the Window Shop, a task not undertaken since the shop began in 1939. Should it be a holding operation to continue to employ the fifteen or so old employees, the executive committee wondered in April 1966, or should it embark on a new venture? The committee questioned whether the Scholarship Fund was performing a unique function in supporting part-time students. And harking back to the Window Shop's original purpose, the committee wrote, "It is clear at the moment that we cannot continue to help 'new Americans,' since there are so few, and with the recent changes in the immigration laws, there will be even fewer in the foreseeable future."[39] These questions remained unanswered as the Window Shop struggled on, and the dinner business continued its slide.

Complaints began trickling in from customers about the declining quality of restaurant meals. Longtime Restaurant employees missed their personal connections with Mrs. Broch, and some may have found Mary Mohrer's crisp professionalism and her suggestions for change in their work patterns, products, or methods hard to accept. In a continuing conflict between Mary and a senior employee, an executive committee report said, "It may have been too difficult for [the employee] to adjust to the change from Mrs. Broch's system of giving massive doses of love to Miss Mohrer's more direct approach."[40]

Staffing the kitchen and Restaurant was an additional challenge. Previously, workers helped out where needed—waitresses often helped in the kitchen—but the executive committee was emphatic in its belief that responsibility for the two operations must be kept separate.[41] In addition, it was difficult to find employees willing to close the Restaurant in the evening and to supervise cleaning operations. The executive committee suggested contacting some "Negro organizations" to see if they had any people who could take responsibility, pointing out that at the moment, the Window Shop had "no Negroes in supervisory positions."[42]

The Bakery had its own unique problems. It could not increase its business because no one found a way to balance its labor intensity and the cost of high-priced ingredients with selling prices that customers would accept. Long-term employees had performed extraordinarily well considering their initial inexperience. They were proud of their accomplishments, but they lacked the background to recognize the impact of changes in Harvard Square, and they did not search for alternative ways of maintaining quality control or for changes in ingredients. Many long-timers were nearly ready to retire and were replaced by young restaurant workers with a different work ethic and no knowledge of the culture of the Window Shop, now approaching its thirtieth year.

In February 1966, the executive committee discussed a proposed buying trip by Mary Mohrer to visit designers in Greece, Israel, and other countries. Recognizing the changed environment in Harvard Square, the committee understood that the Window Shop's once-unique merchandise now had serious competitors in its own backyard; while it approved the trip, it discussed timing and staff coverage in her absence.

By the time Mary returned, rumors were flying that the Window Shop was not doing well, and morale in the Restaurant was understandably low—the employees felt that "management has been weak."[43] Board members were worried. They expressed renewed concern about the purposes of the shop in an era of very little immigration and wondered what role it should play in the "new Cambridge" that now surrounded it. They agreed on one key point: "That the shop has fulfilled its original objective to employ and train everyone."[44] The *raison d'être* of the shop in the late '60s was unclear, and as it became the subject of civilized and extensive debate at board meetings, the Window Shop carried on in the face of mounting problems.

Meanwhile, Mary tried to solve some of the Restaurant's problems and restore some level of profitability. She brought the very basic issue of "poor food," as she called it, to the attention of the kitchen supervisor, Anne Glace, and the chef, Henry Wurmfeld. As a result, the chef agreed to concentrate on those dishes he prepared well and to limit the menu to the Continental specialties that had long been the Restaurant's signature offerings.[45] Weekly buffet luncheons were introduced with special dishes artistically presented; these were a success and contributed to a modest rise in profits.

At this point, the board's emphasis was on seeking the advice of consultants in kitchen design or more broadly, those who could identify a niche in the restaurant business. These short-term advisers were, of necessity, successful American managers who had little experiential knowledge of the Window Shop's culture. This was similar to the board's and the long-term employees' lack of experience with a new generation of customers whose tastes and expectations differed from those of their elders. The executive committee had worked long and effectively on the social services aspects of the shop, but liaison with the business community was not a priority until serious and recurring problems emerged. The consultants cost thousands of dollars in fees, leaving some board members questioning the advisability of engaging them and wondering if the money could have been better spent. A survey by one of the restaurant consultants cost $6,000 and "did not uncover very much that we did not already know."[46]

The board was convinced that the Window Shop needed major renovations to ensure greater efficiency in both the Restaurant and Gift Shop. The kitchen was completely remodeled and updated, and the dining rooms were all painted white, an expenditure of approximately $80,000. Because the Window Shop was closed for a week for renovations, the month of March 1968 was termed "financially disastrous." The next few months saw more customers returning to the Restaurant, however, and the innovation of a Friday night buffet was a success.

But the ups and downs of the restaurant business continued to plague the shop. If there was one successful month, it was followed by two dismal ones. By the fall of 1968, a further decline in lunch and dinner customers was noted, and a new resolve to improve the quality of meals was voiced. Recognizing the need to strengthen the kitchen management, the executive committee gave Mrs. Glace, the kitchen supervisor, more authority. Once again, the committee reviewed the purposes of the Window Shop: "to employ people who could not find employment elsewhere and to provide scholarships." The committee recognized that these two purposes conflicted [since increased payroll costs reduced the funds available for scholarships], but it felt that the Restaurant provided a training opportunity and, as such, it was a service that should be continued.[47]

Once again the urgent need to clarify lines of authority among Restaurant, Bakery and kitchen employees, managers, and the executive committee was apparent. Employees' and managers' responsibilities were often unclear and overlapping. In response, restaurant consultant John Stokes was interviewed in December 1968, with a mandate to reorganize the operation and promote greater efficiency (and to try to improve the still-inferior food). When he was hired, an executive committee member informed Mr. Stokes of the Window Shop's employment tradition, explaining that "we will not be interested in firing somewhat inadequate people, as they are a part of our operation."[48]

This unusual philosophy in a highly competitive business environment set the Window Shop apart from its competitors and undoubtedly contributed to its ultimate downfall.

Stokes hired Jack K. Vissell as manager of the Restaurant, but after several months, the number of dinner customers continued to decline. At the end of 1969 a stark letter to Window Shop employees announced, "There will be no Christmas [bonus] checks this year" because of dwindling profits.

The executive committee, in addition to worrying about restoring the flagging restaurant business, continued to examine its goals and concluded that only the Scholarship Fund (the Ulich Fund) was providing a useful community service. "This presents a philosophical as well as a fiscal problem for us all," wrote Board

President Marion Bever. "The philanthropic purpose of the Window Shop was all-pervading in the '30s and '40s. This basic purpose has now retreated into the activities of the scholarship committee. With two unprofitable years behind us, can we still qualify as a self-supporting philanthropy? We surely cannot continue to support the Ulich Fund out of capital indefinitely. If we are to go forward, we must find ways to operate the Window Shop at a profit. Profitability is now crucial both to our survival as a business and to our qualification as a charity."[49]

At the beginning of 1970, Mary Mohrer reported a $3,000 increase in sales at the bakery counter and "somewhat higher" customer numbers for tea. However, in her opinion, food standards had not improved, personnel problems continued, and the kitchen received an unfavorable grade in a Cambridge Health Department inspection.[50] Despite the best efforts of consultants and new managers and earnest discussions about the future by the executive committee, the Window Shop continued adrift. Even the Gift Shop was suffering: "The clothes department shows a devastating drop in sales," Mary reported. "This is due to less cash available and mostly, I think, to the mini-midi-maxi [hemline] controversy. We are trying to handle more imports, which gives us a better markup, more unusual merchandise, but all this has not really helped us to stem the tide."[51]

Later in 1970, Mary, exhausted and discouraged by the demands of her overwhelming double job, submitted her resignation as general manager. "It is with great relief that I resign as general manager of the Window Shop," she wrote. "I shall now devote all my energy to the Dress and Gift Shop and try to make it as successful as possible in these troubled times."[52]

While the Restaurant struggled, the Gift Shop reported an "excellent month in December 1970, with remarkable sales in jewelry and clothing, and the French yo-yo craze that attracted customers who bought more expensive items."[53] With the exception of a few outstanding months, the decline of the Restaurant inevitably affected the Gift Shop by failing to draw customers as it had done in happier days.

Several managers from well-known Boston restaurants were asked to assess the Window Shop's operation and offer advice. Two of them said the Restaurant's sales volume of $433,000 was indeed respectable, but labor costs were too high. With this volume, they said, the Restaurant should have a profit of approximately 10 percent, or $40,000. It was thought that a liquor license would help to reach and surpass this goal. Another manager revealed that his restaurant's sales volume of about $550,000 was not much more than the Window Shop's, but his business had half as many employees. These advisers also found that the Window Shop's chef "simply had no experience" as a chef.[54]

All the restaurant consultants stressed the importance of hiring an experienced manager, preferably an older person, who could be firm with employees who had developed habits of sloppiness and poor service, and who knew "how to reach a reasonable profit without sacrificing quality."[55]

A new restaurant manager, Guy Greco, was hired in November 1970 and tried to restore the Window Shop's flagging reputation. He worked with individual employees to upgrade their skills and blamed the Window Shop's inability to attract competent staff on its inadequate unemployment insurance and its minimal contributions to health insurance. A budget subcommittee was asked to examine both charges and to increase these expenditures. At the end of February 1971, Henry Beauvais became the new chef, replacing Henry Wurmfeld, who had taken another position.

The Window Shop was not alone in its struggle to survive. It was reported that 1970 and 1971 were difficult years in the restaurant business, with many area restaurants declaring bankruptcy.[56] In one year, from August 1970 to August 1971, the Window Shop lost $50,000. The last few years had been so fraught that the executive committee and the full board questioned the Window Shop's *raison d'être* with increasing urgency. In May 1971, Board President Marion Bever wrote of her concern:

> The original purpose of the Window Shop has largely disappeared. There are still a few employees who fit into the original category; also the Restaurant employs needy students, especially in the summer. The Window Shop has been forced to adopt the attitude of not how many we can afford to employ but how few can do the work efficiently.[57]

Ultimately, the winds of change would destroy the Window Shop. The board members were clearly conflicted. While the budget committee was empowered to draw up a reorganization plan that involved layoffs, other board members discussed marketing plans, such as promoting the *Linzer torte* as a Christmas item for mailing. At a notable board meeting on October 18, 1971, the new president, Richard Kahan, a professor at Harvard Business School, presented in detail the Window Shop's precarious finances and urged the board to act. After reviewing a cash flow estimate from September 1971 through December 1972, the board voted to apply for a $30,000 bank loan for no less than fourteen months. It would be used to defray current payables, severance pay commitments, and interim cash needs, and to support the Scholarship Fund.

Moreover, the board voted to change the format of the Restaurant to a café, serving only beverages, sandwiches, and desserts, and occupying only the first floor of the Restaurant. The second floor vacated by the Restaurant would be rented, preferably to office tenants. In accordance with these decisions, the

Restaurant closed on October 23, 1971, and the Window Shop Café opened three days later.

A year later, the Window Shop was still deeply in the red, with a $28,000 loss by the fall of 1972, and a $20,000 bank loan due in December. At a board of directors meeting on October 11, 1972, the budget committee recommended that the business operations of the Window Shop be terminated "in view of [its] severe and constant losses." In November, the board discussed alternative uses of the Window Shop assets, which included sale of the property to interested Cambridge investors, or sale or lease to a not-for-profit organization, preferably one with a broadly similar mission to that of the Window Shop. To make the latter option possible, a special meeting of the board was called to amend the Window Shop charter to give the corporation the power "to relieve and assist the poor and needy, including refugees from other countries, and to further education; and in connection therewith to operate a restaurant and bakery, to grant scholarships, and to make distributions or otherwise assist or contribute to charitable or educational organizations that qualify as exempt organizations ..."[58] Some board members thought this sounded much like the old Window Shop, hanging on to its belief in the program of thirty-three years.

In December 1972, the Window Shop was sold to the Cambridge Center for Adult Education, a respected part of the Cambridge community, for $310,000. It had been incorporated in April 1876 as the Cambridge Social Union, and in 1889 had purchased and moved into the historic Brattle House, built by William Brattle in 1727. Located at 42 Brattle Street, a block away from the Window Shop's home, the Brattle House was exquisitely maintained and contributed much to the ambience of Harvard Square.

The sale was a propitious move for both organizations. It gave all Window Shop supporters, customers, and employees delight that such an appropriate Cambridge neighbor would be the new owner and caretaker. The Cambridge Center found the space it needed for expansion nearby for its students and staff. It renamed the Window Shop building the Blacksmith House, but echoes of the shop remained. In the entrance foyer is a brass plaque honoring Alice Perutz Broch, and a classroom bears the name of Elsa Brändström Ulich. Both Brattle Street houses are preserved by the center as "living museums" and are listed in the National Register of Historic Places.

The Cambridge Center took on responsibility for the Bakery, which was still operating, agreeing to employ its workers until they reached retirement. Doris Martin, the longtime protégée of Alice Broch, continued as head baker until 1995, and Pearl Morrison staffed the Bakery counter until 1996, when the Bakery ceased to exist.

Board President Richard Kahan, in a letter to employees, announced the closing of the Window Shop after thirty-three years: "While the WS is closing as a
gift shop and café, it will not end but will carry on as a Foundation to provide
scholarships and aid to the deserving and needy. Our ability to do so has been
enhanced and in fact made possible by your successful efforts in building an
organization from scratch to the position where we now stand: able to sell a valuable property to the Cambridge Adult Education Center [sic]."[59] Various board
members made valiant efforts to ensure that valued employees were treated fairly
in regard to severance pay and the shop's pension plan.

A letter to board members from Mary Mohrer and Gift Shop employees Ilse
Heyman, Tamar Wurmfeld, and Denise Serres expressed the sadness of all
employees:

> Now that the end of the Window Shop is coming closer and your last
> meeting is approaching, I would like to express to all of you what the
> Window Shop meant to me and all of us.
>
> It was a gathering place in Cambridge where foreign and domestic
> clothes were sold and where the best of domestic and foreign crafts were
> shown. The Shop was a valuable center for weavers, potters, and jewelry
> designers. Many a fine craftsman received his first order at the Window
> Shop. Back of all activities was always the thought that human profits
> and not just money profits count.
>
> In its early days, its social place was of foremost importance. This did
> not mean learning a trade or selling your crafts. It meant a spiritual
> ground where one's life roots produced new sprouts again. It was the
> most wonderful teamwork of people from different countries, different
> backgrounds, who all contributed to the whole. Many of you were part
> of it and with the help of the Cambridge community helped to achieve
> this.
>
> For us it was a way of life, and we loved it.
>
> Out of the old purpose had grown a new one. The Window Shop had
> become an institution, important to the community. It was beautiful in
> ever so many ways and would have been well worth saving.
>
> We know that you tried and are sorry that you did not succeed.
>
> We all are very sad to see it go and are very proud to have been part of
> it. We hope you are too. [60]

The employees' sorrow was matched by that of many loyal customers, who wrote of their feeling of great loss and in some cases anger that this special place that occupied such an important place in their hearts would soon vanish.

Dorothy Dahl, board president from 1964 to 1968 and head of the Scholarship Fund after the Window Shop closed, shared her thoughts on this painful final chapter:

> The generation of women who began the Window Shop remained its prime movers until things became intractable. The men on the early board were welcome colleagues, who had expertise in finance, business (both in manufacturing and retail), law and national refugee problems. As profits declined, the women turned to the men—the experts—when they needed to incorporate, or for the move to 56 Brattle Street when they needed advice on purchasing real estate and financing it. This time experts were needed in the arcane world of restaurant management, outside the board's ken. The board hired American consultants who were from another generation, but not directly knowledgeable about the early 1930s through World War II, and the heart-stopping upheaval of families in that long time span.
>
> For the women on the board in the late sixties and early seventies, what had earlier been a joyful and gratifying experience turned out to be frustrating and, finally, incomprehensible. Employees who had been loving and loyal had become anxious, uncertain of their future. Board members, most of whom lacked work experience, were unable to understand the reality of this situation.
>
> Executive committee members worked long and sometimes feverishly to make certain that details of the retirement plan and Social Security benefits could support employees when a decision to close the Window Shop seemed inevitable. The amounts for each plan, while helpful, were woefully inadequate for long-term employees, so central to the Window Shop's success. Committee members reached out to friends and acquaintances who could help long-term employees find suitable jobs, but success was sporadic. The anguish of both groups was palpable.[61]

Alice Cope, one of the Window Shop's most devoted and inspirational leaders, said:

> Many people have asked me why the Window Shop was closed. It is very hard to explain, because so many were hurt, and dwelling on the

past does no good. All that can be said is that the Restaurant was losing money. The board made efforts to rescue it, but couldn't....[62]

Ordinary business methods were instituted where only extraordinary methods had been successful before. They all failed because the special ingredients which had made the Shop such a success were no longer understood.

At the end of 1972, the Board of Directors reluctantly decided to close the entire Shop. The work which those imaginative women had set out to do in 1939 was completed.[63]

Voices

"In the last weeks people came in: 'Why didn't you tell us? We could have raised $10,000, $100,000.' Well, maybe yes, maybe no. But why didn't they come earlier? Why didn't they buy more? They liked our merchandise. It's all very easy then to feel sad and upset and sorry. But it was too late."

Ilse Heyman

"I was in Harvard Square one day and someone yelled to me from across the street: 'What do you think you're doing, closing the Window Shop?' She was very angry."

Hedy Sturges

The Scholarship Fund

Board President Richard Kahan's hope, expressed in his letter to employees about the closing of the Window Shop, was that the shop would continue to operate as a "Foundation to provide scholarships and aid to the deserving and the needy." Anne Harken became the succeeding president of the board and worked with some members to make a new scholarship program that would be available to the same category of students as those who had been helped by the Ulich Fund. They believed that funding could come from invested proceeds from the sale of 56 Brattle Street, continuing gifts from old Window Shop customers and friends who had contributed to the Ulich Fund, and from other sources they could find in the area. The new scholarship fund would retain the structure of the Window Shop Board; it was renamed the Window Shop, Inc. Scholarship Fund, so that its identification would be clear. The additional line, "formerly the Elsa Brändström Ulich Fund," was a nostalgic reminder of earlier days and a major figure in the shop's history.

Some personal stories by scholarship recipients will serve to indicate the diversity and the incredible quality of these latest beneficiaries of the fund. These stories and others were used in Scholarship Fund appeal letters in the 1980s.

A thirty-year-old Vietnamese engineering student began his voyage toward graduate work in America by remodeling a river banana boat measuring seventy-two by fifteen feet. He transported himself and 419 others from a town near Ho Chi Minh City to East Malaysia and into the custody of the United Nations Commissioner for Refugees. He was transferred to a refugee camp on Pappen Island run by the International Red Cross and finally came to Boston under the sponsorship of the International Rescue Committee. He is now [1981] a student at Boston University School of Engineering, working twenty hours a week and, perhaps not surprisingly, gets A's.

This is a letter expressing my utmost gratitude to you and your fellow Committee members for all the financial assistance you gave me towards my college tuition.... I am from Uganda, East Africa, attending Pharmacy School at Northeastern University. With the much help you gave me, I was able to graduate in time this September with my Bachelor's Degree in Pharmacy, passed my Licensing Board exams, and two days ago became a Registered Pharmacist. I have accepted a job with Rite-Aid [a retail drug chain], and they have offered me a great salary, good benefits, and a great atmosphere to work in.... I therefore greatly emphasize my great appreciation for all your assistance, without which I would not accomplish what I have today. Thank you very much.

A loan was granted to an Iranian student whose father had been put in jail and could no longer send him money. He had almost finished his course at Northeastern University in Mathematics and Computer Science. He not only repaid his loan soon after graduation, but made a sizeable contribution so that the Fund could help others.

A young blind woman, a Palestinian Christian from Israel, received a loan. She needed additional training and earned a Master's Degree in Counseling at Boston University's School of Allied Health Services. She is now [1982] a counselor to the blind at the North Suffolk Mental Health Association in East Boston. This student repaid her loan in full. A few weeks ago she became a U.S. citizen, of which she is very proud.

A brilliant young cellist, a student at the Moscow Conservatory, in 1983 made his way to the United States. With the help of an international refugee organization, he came to Boston where he had no funds, no friends, no introductions. In desperation, he turned to "Musical Instruction" in the Yellow Pages of the telephone directory. With remarkable luck, he reached a member of the Boston Symphony Orchestra, who was so impressed with the young man's talent and credentials that he introduced him to a local university. He was accepted as a student with the understanding that somehow his tuition would be paid. The Window Shop Scholarship Fund stepped in and helped this young musician to finish his education. In time he will no doubt make a contribution to the musical life of this country.

Some veteran board members stepped forward to help in this new venture: Lillian Cohan Levin gave the scholarship students access to what became known as "Lil's magic closet," a space in her home where students could come to select new clothes from her family's clothing business, a real boost after their usual thrift-shop shopping. Throughout the life of the new fund, Gisela Wyzanski stayed active to give her expert advice and to write fundraising appeal letters. Deborah Hermann, an experienced social worker, continued to interview students as she had for the Ulich Fund. Marion Bever assisted Anne Harken, the new president, in recruiting new and younger women to be interviewers and new board members. These eight new women[64] were surprisingly similar to the original Harvard faculty wives who had started the Window Shop in 1939, mostly faculty wives from MIT and Harvard, their interest in students serious and their manner easy.

Mrs. Harken recruited Alice Bradford Hall for the board. She was affiliated with the International Institute of Boston and was an expert on immigration and the arcane details of seeking political asylum, whether for citizenship or only for education. Her knowledge of the kaleidoscope of world events and their effects on the regulations faced by students was total.

Slowly the group developed new "rules," principally limitations on which students they could help and what sort of help they could give. In its waning years, the Ulich Fund received only half as many requests for financial assistance as it had in earlier years, and the consensus for the new fund was that "financial assistance" be dropped, except for children of Window Shop employees. Giving awards only to undergraduates seemed fair, since graduate students often had access to resources that were not available to undergraduates. Four-year colleges were preferred to two-year ones, and the committee was disinclined, as had been the Ulich Fund, to give for the first undergraduate year. Relatives of Window Shop employees, however, were always special cases.

"Rules" were understood as "priorities," and interviewers were consistently aware of the special situation of the specific student before them for this one particular year. It was tempting to give some priority to those who wished to become American citizens, or who discovered once they were in the United States that they couldn't go home again. Compelling arguments were made for those from small countries in Africa, for example, who hoped to return and use their education for the good of their country. There were still some true refugee families that might include a college-bound student. The variations were endless, and the needs were great. For the older board members, these considerations were familiar from earlier decades; to newcomers to the board, discussions of these issues made them feel they were part of a tradition. Scholarship Fund interviewers could offer advice, keep in touch with the student's university, and make referrals that might be helpful.

Word spread that this new Window Shop Scholarship Fund was the only one in the Boston area that was prepared to offer help to foreign-born students other than Window Shop refugees or their children. Although the amount of an individual award ranged from five or six hundred up to one thousand dollars, it was calculated to make the difference (as had the Ulich Fund) that would enable a student, after all, to make it through a year of education. Sometimes part of the award was in the form of a loan, if there was a realistic belief that repayment was possible in the foreseeable future, but no form was devised to formalize it. Most interviewers were pleased by repayments when they came, and easy about it when they did not. The way of working with individual students was labor intensive for the interviewers, but profoundly interesting.

There were things the committee would not do: pay student debts, consider awards if other resources were readily available, or fund scholarships if the program the student desired could be completed less expensively elsewhere. If the committee felt the student was not "up" to the program proposed and could be encouraged to try something else, or if the student's needs were so great that help became unrealistic, funds were denied.

In early 1979, Dorothy Dahl, a board member since 1955 and board president from 1964 to 1968, returned from India and was asked by the nominating committee to be president of the Scholarship Fund Board. She had been out of the country during the painful years before 1972 and came back to the group eager to help with this new and exciting project. Anne Harken continued to run the scholarship committee with intelligence and flair as its chairman.

Mrs. Dahl asked Joseph T. Lambie to become treasurer. Lambie had taught history at Wellesley College and then moved to Loomis, Sayles as a financial investor and adviser with great success. His years of experience did wonders for Window Shop investments. He helped to arrange supplementary retirement funds for the shop's two managers and produced funds for needed scholarships. His attitude toward the money from the sale of the Window Shop to the Cambridge Center for Adult Education was less hidebound than that of most bankers, who abhorred using anything more than the interest from assets. Lambie was aware, from his previous volunteer activity in an organization devoted to low-income clients, that often their needs were serious enough to seek a balance between saving capital for the future or filling needs in the present. Thus, in a careful way, some capital could be withdrawn from successful investments to cover real needs for deserving persons. No one knew better than the Window Shop interviewers how much difference a relatively small amount of money for a scholarship could make to a life. At the end of one of these discussions, a board member said, "The committee believes that the future can be overemphasized."[65]

Another concern before the board was documenting the Window Shop story so that future historians could study not only its response to a historic catastrophe, but also how it adapted to changing circumstances, while keeping the aim of the institution squarely on helping deserving people. In the mid-eighties, a concerted effort was made to interview as many employees, customers, and board members as possible, and everyone was asked to rummage in their files and attics for minutes of meetings, letters, notes, recipes, and anecdotes. Some members hunted for the recipes they knew would be of interest, a difficult task because the amounts of the ingredients were in gargantuan sizes, and all knowledgeable cooks or bakers needed time to experiment to reduce the ingredients to a more accept-able number, like six or eight portions.

As mentioned in the Preface, placing the archival material in the Arthur and Elizabeth Schlesinger Library on the History of Women in America at Radcliffe College, which today is part of the Radcliffe Institute for Advanced Study at Harvard University, was entirely appropriate. Spiritually, the Radcliffe Institute is a close neighbor of the Window Shop in Harvard Square, and most importantly, the archives are available to the public.

By the mid-1980s, board members were getting grayer and finding they had less energy than before. It slowly became clear that any new members to be recruited would also be in their sixties and seventies, not in their thirties and for-ties, the ages when these particular women had become interested in volunteer work. Young women now at that age were well along in a paid profession and had no time for intensive volunteer work. The board came to a consensus to ensure that the fund's capital continued to be used to help students from foreign coun-tries, many of whom were planning to become citizens just as their predecessors in the late 1930s had done. The continuity, however, would have to come from institutions rather than from individuals. After lengthy discussions, assisted by longtime board activists such as Alice Cope, plans to dissolve the organization and disburse its funds were finalized in December 1986.

The group began by making a onetime, taxable distribution to the old Window Shop employees, who, after all, had made the money the board was dis-bursing. Constance Cox, a board member who had been active on such distribu-tions at the time the shop closed in 1972, returned to give her expertise in dividing one-quarter of the total amount among the few (but very special) people who were covered by the Window Shop's meager retirement plan.

Further, a decision was made to place a Window Shop scholarship at Northeastern University in Boston, since its Cooperative Plan had been a great help to Ulich Fund and Scholarship Fund recipients over the years. In addition, a contribution to the Schlesinger Library would help with the cataloguing and care of the Window Shop papers. Sixty percent went to the Boston Foundation, whose Access Program helps inner-city young people get through college. The program begins in junior high school and includes special services and counseling throughout. The gift was earmarked for foreign-born students in the Access Program, thus providing a degree of continuity with the earlier work of the fund.

During its fifteen-year existence, the Scholarship Fund posted some astonish-ing numbers. In this period, nearly $400,000 had been granted to 922 applicants between 1972 and 1987. This came from the investment income from the sale of the Window Shop property, annual contributions from loyal Window Shop supporters, modest contributions from capital, and modest repayment of loans by students.

The most arresting figures concerned the countries of origin of the students. A comparison with the twentieth anniversary of the Window Shop in 1959 describes it best. By 1959 nearly 90 percent of the employees and of recipients of the Assistance Fund were from Germany or Austria. The scholarship committee, in its fifteen years of operation, found that the 922 students came from seventy-nine countries, with Africa providing nearly 43 percent of the total. A surprising number of African recipients came from one small country, Eritrea. The next largest number came from the Near East, with Iranians making up nearly half the total (some fled the monarchy; others later fled the Ayatollah Khomeini). Fifteen percent came from Russia, 10.5 percent from Asia, and a third were from Vietnam. The North American continent produced 7.5 percent, the same percentage as Europe. These figures, of course, reflect and underscore the seismic shifts in immigration and history.

Furthermore, the demographics of these scholarship recipients reveal dramatic changes from the 1940s and the Assistance Fund. There were fewer whole-family immigration problems, and when they surfaced, as they did with the Russian families who began arriving in the 1970s, there were no Window Shop services to help. Because the Restaurant/Bakery and Gift Shop had closed, no jobs with flexible hours could be offered immigrants, no assistance in acclimatization such as Friendship House was available, and no well-organized referral system for social services in the Boston area was offered, such as had been provided by the Window Shop. By the time the Scholarship Fund ended, students no longer lived or attended school mainly in Cambridge, as they had in the early days of the fund, but were spread out over the Greater Boston area and the Commonwealth of Massachusetts.

Dorothy Dahl shares this reminiscence:

> When the Cambridge Center for Adult Education made its final payment to the Scholarship Fund in December 1987, they hosted a gala reception to honor their mortgage burning and the entire joint enterprise. All representatives of the Window Shop and the Cambridge Center, and a few friends from the city of Cambridge, gathered to toast thirty-three years of the Window Shop and fifteen years of the Scholarship Fund—a surprising total of forty-eight years of assistance to people from nearly every country in the world from a mixture of volunteers, students, new Americans, and employees—a unique mix of wonderful and decent people.

Lunch under the umbrellas, circa 1958.

Epilogue

More than one generation of Cambridge and Boston-area residents, students, parents, and tourists have grown up without the Window Shop on Brattle Street. "I'll meet you at Starbucks" does not carry the same cachet as "I'll meet you at the Window Shop" did for three decades. A rendezvous at the Window Shop carried with it the promise of meeting friends over delicious pastry and fine coffee, enjoying European cuisine, and shopping for extraordinary gifts and clothing.

While the good tastes—both in food and in merchandise—are now a part of the past, the Window Shop leaves a unique history that transcends fond remembrances of *Linzer torte* and handcrafted jewelry.

The determined, resilient women who founded the organization had no plan to guide them, no model for starting a business, no work experience outside their homes. Similarly, the refugee women had never been employed and had no plan other than survival, but they brought to the enterprise their talents, skills, intelligence, and optimism. They ran the day-to-day operation and, with the board members, offered new refugees a step up in the new world, and, most important, employment.

The primary legacy of the Window Shop is the success that these disparate groups of women achieved through their courage, vision, and strength: the creation of a unique organization that helped thousands of refugees while building a tradition in Cambridge that has never been duplicated.

Most of the Window Shop refugees became American citizens. In 1974, former Board President Alice Cope wrote:

> The contributions to the United States of the New Americans and the cultural changes which took place because of them are extraordinary. If one adds up the influence of architects, psychiatrists, writers, philosophers, educators, physicists and musicians among the newcomers, it is absolutely staggering what they gave to their new country.[66]

Deep friendships took root here and blossomed; many of them have endured until the present day. High standards were set, both in the Restaurant/Bakery, which insisted on the finest ingredients even under wartime restrictions, and in the Gift and Dress Shop, where a talented buyer selected merchandise that her loyal customers appreciated and purchased. Hundreds of scholarship recipients made their way in life thanks to the Window Shop.

"The Window Shop grew and prospered at a time when American women mostly expected to be 'at home,'" Dorothy Dahl summarized. "Their newfound ability and consistency was the wonder, as was their belief that anything was possible if there were an authentic need to fill."

While the Window Shop was a product uniquely of its time, it lives in memory and now in print as a model for a community working together to help refugees, irrespective of their country of origin. Whenever people of good will reach out to help needy immigrants, and especially when they help them to become benefactors as well as beneficiaries, they are, in effect, following in the footsteps of the Window Shop.

Four

Portraits

The Refugees

Following are portraits in words and, where available, in photographs, of the refugees who helped shape the Window Shop. This section is followed by portraits of board members.

Lotte Benfey

Lotte Benfey in the Window Shop garden.

Together with Elisabeth Martens, Mrs. Benfey managed the Window Shop Restaurant under the direction of Alice Perutz Broch from 1945 to 1964.

She was born Lotte Maria Ullstein on December 25, 1900, in Berlin. She studied pediatric nursing and in 1923 married Eduard Benfey, Chief Justice of the Supreme Court of Economic Arbitration in the Weimar Republic until the Nazi takeover. They fled Germany in 1939, entered the United States in 1940, and became U.S. citizens in 1945.

In their early American years, the Benfeys operated Goodwill House, a refugee guest house in Groton, Massachusetts. In 1945 Mrs. Benfey became an assistant manager of the Window Shop Restaurant and was known as a strict but fair supervisor. Pearl Morrison, a waitress at the time, said, "Mrs. Benfey was very particular about everything. Everybody had to have their aprons starched, white and clean, neatly ironed uniforms. On occasion she sent people home if they didn't have clean uniforms. And she always saw to it that if you needed extra hours, she would try to squeeze in half an hour here or there so you could make a few extra dollars and at the same time be beneficial to the Shop."

Mrs. Benfey's eagle eye for detail was legendary. Pearl Morrison tells of setting up all the tables for lunch and being satisfied that she was done. "Then Mrs. Benfey entered the dining room, and said, 'I see a fork missing on the back table.' It was amazing because out of all of the thirty-six tables, she spied the fork that was missing on this one table. That shocked me, and that was something I never forgot!"

Ilse Heyman, assistant manager of the Gift Shop, remembers Mrs. Benfey as:

> This stately lady, very tall, thin as a stick. I imagine that's how she always was. Her husband was much shorter than she was, and he was also much older. He was a friend of her father's. Mrs. Benfey always wore navy blue or gray suits; she saw everything, she knew everything. She was very concerned with the well-being of her waitresses, and the waitresses loved her. She was a lady. Her hair was pulled back in a bun, and she had high cheekbones, the classic Slavic face. Her husband used to come at three o'clock and do the cash boxes after lunch was over. That was his contribution. They were from Berlin, but he had been high up in the government. He was not Jewish. She was related to the Ullstein publishing house, and they were Jewish, so I guess that's why they came [to America]....
>
> "She was a classic. To her it really didn't matter what your background was. It wasn't important—you only dealt with nice people. People were people, and she really took care of them as well as she could. She would see that there was a fork missing, but she was never nasty about it."

"Mrs. Benfey was something straight out of Europe," recalled Board Member Hedy Sturges. "Absolutely! Her thin figure—I'll never forget it—overlooking the whole scene. She had all her workers lined up, hairnets and all, and she just had this wonderful way about her."

Mrs. Benfey died on May 13, 1987, at Friends Homes in Greensboro, North Carolina.

Alice Boehm

Alice Boehm was the Window Shop's consummate dressmaker, whose dirndl creations put the Window Shop on the map. Ilse Heyman, assistant manager of the Gift and Dress Shop, remembers her:

> My first encounter with Alice Boehm occurred on the day that the Window Shop celebrated its move to 56 Brattle Street, in April 1947, with an open house for friends and workers.
>
> Alice Boehm was a very handsome, charming woman, with a ready smile, beautifully dressed in her own creations. She delivered some dirndls, and I handed her new fabric for new orders. The dirndl craze was in full swing by then, and Litzi (as I soon called her) and I began a

cooperation that lasted for years. We also chuckled many times about the bizarre requests of some of our customers. She had a wonderful sense of humor, and her intuition of how a garment should fit even if she never saw the customer was uncanny. Slowly I started to send her some of our customers whose figures did not fit into our manufactured clothes, but I always asked Litzi for permission to do so. Many of these women became her loyal customers and friends for life.

Litzi and I became good friends when I asked her to join me in a concert series, which we enjoyed until she became ill. Together with Mary Mohrer, Litzi was the reason for the early success of the Gift and Dress Shop. They did the designing together, but it was Litzi's fine workmanship and ideas that helped Mary to get the Shop off its feet.

The comments below are by Mrs. Boehm's nephew Chris Brandt and were delivered at her funeral:

Alice E. Boehm died on August 14, 2003, but the important fact is that she lived for ninety-four years. She was born Alice Elizabeth Hirschmann in Vienna, Austria, on August 9, 1909. The Hirschmann family, who changed their name to Brandt in 1933, managed to escape the Nazi regime during late 1938 and the first half of 1939, fleeing in three shifts. Alice and her mother took what turned out to be the most dangerous and difficult route into exile, traveling by train across Germany to Cologne. A border closing stranded them, and Quakers in Cologne hid them until they could make it to Holland.

Once the entire family had made it to the United States, they came first to Boston, then moved to the Seattle area, but Alice, her husband, Jula Boehm, and her parents soon returned to settle permanently in the more congenial and Old World atmosphere of Cambridge in 1941. There she began to support herself and her parents by making Austrian-style dresses called dirndls for sale through the Window Shop, a cooperative endeavor on Brattle Street, where many refugees managed to eke out a living during the difficult war years. She was divorced after the war, and while continuing to work for the Window Shop, she established a small business out of her residence designing and making fine ladies' clothing. She established a reputation for extremely fine handwork, and for the ability to adapt current styles to real women. She was forced to retire at the age of eighty-eight in 1997 after suffering a stroke.

We will always remember Alice Boehm—Litzi to her family and friends—as a woman of enormous integrity. She worked hard at her trade for seventy-four years, from the time she began helping her mother at the age of twenty-four, and raised her skills by dint of constant practice to the level of an art. The work was the work, whether she was sewing top-of-the-line fabric, showing me how to set sleeves on a shirt, making a gift for a friend, or an apron for herself, and it had to be done properly; she knew all the tricks of the trade, but there was always a right way and a shortcut. I never knew her to take the latter.

She, who never wanted one, had an adventurous life, full of clamor and crisis. Growing up in Vienna during the first World War and the hyperinflation that followed left her with scars that never entirely healed. And growing up Jewish in a city that had both a high number of Jewish professionals and one of the most virulent cases of anti-Semitism in anti-Semitic Europe must have been traumatic. Whatever peace she achieved was richly deserved.

She didn't like talking about the bad times—"The past is the past," she'd say—but once in a while she'd let slip one fragment or another, often an ironic detail. Like the circumstance that the man who drove them to the border and across was a Nazi official who made it clear that his plausible deniability depended on his not knowing who she and her mother were. The image that will always stay with me is of the night she and grandmother stood on the blacked-out deck of a liner in the pitch-dark middle of the English Channel, heading for New York out of Rotterdam, and watched as artillery fire arched up from both sides of the channel and passed above their heads....

Life taught her suffering and never to expect too much. But she never lost her sense of humor. She loved a good joke, and she would listen to the Viennese jokes I'd learned from her brother, my father, over and over and still get the same pleasure from them. But mostly her humor was of the self-deprecating variety; she refused to take herself too seriously. This trait stayed with her even after her illness had robbed her of the power to finish a thought. Once, when I visited her at Belmont, she said suddenly, as if a great insight had come to her, "*Ja, ich glaube das soll man alles ... Wie heist das?*" (for she often spoke German and English interchangeably then). "Yes, I believe one must ... How do you say that? *Weisst du*, when you go to ... What I want to say is ... *Was wollte ich sagen?*" and the thought trailed off. "Oh well, what does it matter?" When I nodded and encouraged her to go on, she asked, "How do you mean that?" And then when I said I didn't know because I didn't know what she wanted to say, she nodded thoughtfully. "Yes, I think we do not know ourselves at all, but I would really like to ask." "What do you want to ask?" I responded, and she looked at me with surprise and a mischievous smile as she replied, "Good question!"

Quietly she went about making the world a better place for those of us fortunate enough to have been part of her circle. In remembering her we would profit by her example, and learn to leave the world a little better than we found it. So, we celebrate a thoughtful and sensitive life, a woman who transcended the ugliness of her times to create beauty wherever she could.

Alice Perutz Broch

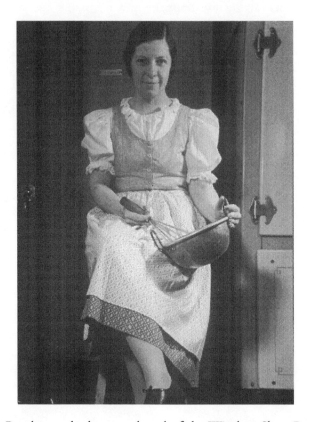

Alice Perutz Broch was the heart and soul of the Window Shop Restaurant and Bakery. She and her partner Olga Schiffer first thought of starting a Tea Room and made it happen. The Restaurant and Bakery on Brattle Street was their creation as well. Its early success rested on Mrs. Broch's shoulders, and it became her legacy. As a board member wrote, "She did it all with charm, brains, and a remarkable sense of others and a wish to be of service to them."

She was enormously capable, a gifted cook, and equally important, she was in today's terms "a people person." She cared for the wounded souls who fled from Hitler's persecution, she knew everyone at the Window Shop and their family members, and she was completely devoted to the enterprise. More than anyone else, she and Mary Mohrer were the Window Shop.

Mrs. Broch's achievements are even more remarkable in light of her background: she lived a privileged life in Vienna, with household cooks and servants—until the Nazi takeover of Austria forced her to flee to the United States with her son. With no experience in cooking or baking, she taught herself the art of making Viennese pastry and later took culinary classes to perfect her art.

We have only personal notes and letters (and countless recipes) from Mrs. Broch today—she was not interviewed in the 1980s with other Window Shop employees, since she had left the area when she retired in 1964. Nonetheless, she lives in the loving memories of her family and coworkers. She died in Dallas, Texas, in 1999 at the age of 101.

Voices

"My mother, then Alice Perutz, was divorced from my father, Paul D. Perutz, in 1931 in Vienna.... My father and Edith [his wife] fled Vienna immediately after the Nazi takeover to Holland, and they eventually came to the United States. My brother Fred left Vienna by himself also very early, probably in March 1938. All of us had visas and guarantees from Mr. Eugene Schwabach; without these none of us could have come to the U.S.

"Mother and I left Vienna together for Zurich in July 1938, where we lived for a number of months. Mother took domestic employment in England in the early months of 1939 while I attended school in Reading, England. Mother and I sailed together on the President Roosevelt in April 1939 to the United States.

"After her divorce in Vienna, Mother met Mr. Frederick Broch. He found employment with an engineering firm in Boston, and as a result of this, Mother and I moved to Cambridge in 1939. She married him in 1941, and we all lived together at 21 Wendell Street in Cambridge."

Letter from George Perutz, April 2003

"When Mrs. Perutz and this lovely Mr. Broch got married, it was months before anybody knew anything about it. One day someone said, 'You know, Mrs. Perutz isn't Mrs. Perutz any more. She's Mrs. Broch.' I said, 'What? How did that happen?' So I took myself down to the kitchen and I said, 'What's this about your having gotten married again?' 'Oh,' she said, 'just two old things getting married!'"

Alice Cope

"Mrs. Perutz-Broch's wealth of Old World recipes had been the parting gift of a devoted Viennese family cook, Marie. In commenting on the richness of the ingredients, the old woman remarked that if these recipes were used, her mistress need not know how to cook. It was beyond the power of her imagination to dream that those same recipes would become famous as Window Shop dishes, or that they would start Mrs. Broch on her successful career in this country. Thanks to her knowledge of how good food should taste and her extraordinary under-standing of people, she became, in 1942, the first successful manager of the Restaurant and Bakery."

Anonymous board member, 1949

"After three months of the new management, the treasurer's report showed a substantial profit for the Restaurant and Bakery. In spite of difficult war-time conditions, economies had been managed without upsetting the customers. In fact Mrs. Broch reported that they liked her use of leftovers and the new recipes invented due to food shortages. And the cooperation of the workers—for now it was their shop—was demonstrated when they shopped for butter and brought it to the kitchen instead of to their families. The merchants were showing their interest by trying to see that the Shop didn't lack essential supplies. One day a truck driver for nearby Sage's Market, after his delivery, stood about until Mrs. Broch came near. He said, 'This is a funny crowd—you all talk with an accent.' Mrs. Broch explained who they were, where they came from, and what the Shop meant to them. The next day he brought a pound of butter, which Mr. Sage had given to him as a present, to the 'funny crowd.'"

Alice Cope

"Mrs. Alice Broch, manager of the restaurant, is an Austrian woman who had two sons in the American Army. One is now married; the other at Harvard. Sometimes people ask, she says, whether any Americans are employed by the Window Shop. The answer is to be found right in the kitchen, where an American war veteran is the second cook and another is a kitchen helper. Some of the others in the restaurant also are Americans. All employees are willing to take advice from each other and from interested customers.

"'There is no competition,' says Mrs. Broch. 'We all realize our interdepend-ence. The whole project is democracy in operation. And when we go away on vacations, it is so nice to come back!'"

The Christian Science Monitor, March 23, 1947

"The restaurant's early years were difficult. Broch spent long hours testing European recipes that were prepared in a house nearby and carried over by volun-teers. Broch said the staff came to work at 5 AM because 'many times our cooking would collapse and we had to cook it all over again.' They ate the failures. 'It's a wonder we could digest them. But we were young, hard-working and hungry.'"

The Boston Globe (date unavailable)

"Born in Vienna, Mrs. Broch received the customary liberal arts training, and her only talent, aside from recipe collecting, lay in music. A pianist, she often joined with her family circle and friends in chamber music recitals in her home. Upon coming to this country, she added to her native skill as a cook considerable knowledge of culinary arts gained through a course at a Boston cooking school, and now supervises 64 employees at the Window Shop. She has supplemented her knowledge and training with extension courses in restaurant management taken at Boston University, and all her leisure hours are spent in pursuit of new and more unique recipes."

The Boston Globe, Sept. 30, 1947

"Mrs. Broch was unique. Both Mary Mohrer and Mrs. Broch were well-educated people, and these were people that had good ways of dealing with who-ever they hired. Mary took such an interest in what you wanted—that doesn't mean that you didn't have to work for what was needed, but what was your inter-est in life and what you did. And the same thing was on the other side for Mrs. Broch, and she was a great peacemaker, which is what you needed in the Restaurant! It's not easy, and you come across all kinds of people, and she always tried to defuse the situation that could have gotten volatile, you know, so you didn't have the usual kitchen atmosphere there."

Tamar Wurmfeld

"Her personal attachment to employees began with her first interview: their hopes, plans, family. Next she went to the number of hours they could work, which days, and the money they needed. Only then did details of a work sched-ule for the organization come into play. When she came to the executive com-mittee to suggest changes in arrangements or increases to our always-modest wage scale, her requests were always couched in terms of the individuals affected, their family, the needs, the changes in family plans."

Dorothy Dahl

"I remember looking for an apartment, and the landlord said to me, 'Whom should I call for a reference?' I gave him Mrs. Broch's number and asked him to call her, and he came back to me and said, 'Oh, my, Mrs. Broch said, "Whatever she does I'm personally responsible for it."' I never took the apartment, but just the thought of it....

"She [Mrs. Broch] was there from mornings at eight until six or seven o'clock in the evening. Her heart was with everything, and her aim was to help people. You would never get the feeling that at one time she had servants. She never talked about it, only except for one person, and that was her cook, Marie, where we got some recipes from.

"She was a very good narrator. She could tell stories; she could make them so lively. And downstairs we had this big kitchen, and her office was in the middle of the kitchen. She could see the chefs; when there was a little something going on, she would jump right up and constantly she would say, 'Speak English,' because we had German people there, we also at that time had—which I think was unusual—we had colored people working there. Of course, Mrs. Roosevelt called us 'the United Nations.'

"As a supervisor, she always looked at you not only as a worker, but she also went into your family, your children, in general to know how everything was going, because I think at the board meeting she would say, 'Look, they need help.' She would check on people … really amazing. A wonderful, wonderful woman."

Doris Martin

"After graduation, my college roommate and I traveled in Europe for several months. When my mother told Mrs. Broch that I would be going to Vienna, she asked me if I'd do some tasting for her. She was afraid that after so many years away from the old country, using American ingredients, her Viennese pastries were losing their authenticity. She gave me a list of what to sample. What an assignment! After each bite I'd close my eyes and roll the food around in my mouth. Not once could I detect a shred of difference between Mrs. B.'s baking and Vienna's. She was right on the mark."

Judy Wolfinsohn Parker

"Alice Broch was always good-looking even when she was older, and she was beautiful when she was young. She was certainly very intelligent; she had a good sense of humor, but she came from very different perspectives. As Mary [Mohrer] said, 'My watch is a labor watch,' and Mary always fought for what she felt was your due. Mrs. Broch thought more about your needs. Mary didn't look at needs, but what your work was worth. Mary was a good businesswoman. Mrs. Broch was a peacemaker, which she had to be."

Ilse Heyman

"Mrs. Broch—with everybody in the place, not just Doris and I, but with each and every person—she was into their lives, so that she could comfort them and see that they were happy where they were, to see if they were being taken care of, to see what the Shop was doing for them. You have to be a different type of person to have a job like that. You couldn't be just an ordinary person.

"She said she liked people who really worked hard. But the point was that everybody that knew her had no other choice. They automatically wanted to work hard for her, so it was a mutual situation as far as I could see. You wanted to please her to no end."

Pearl Morrison

"When I started out in the Bakery and Mrs. Broch was still there, a couple of years before she retired, and I would go to her when I had made something and told her the amounts, she would say, 'Oh, we have to charge $18.' I said, 'That's a little bit much.' She said, 'My dear, my dear, you see this here? Out of these $18, here's your salary, here is your uniform, your insurance, the lights …' because I was a greenhorn. And she said, 'Who's going to pay for the light and the electricity, the insurance?' and this is the way I learned. But she wouldn't holler at you or say, 'What do you think?' She'd say, 'My dear, my dear!' And not just to me, to everybody."

Doris Martin

"If the Shop had gone on, if Mrs. Broch had been able to continue, we would have gone into take-out food, because she did it occasionally. She always did two enormous turkeys for the Christmas party that Oliver and I gave each year for the house staff at the Mass. General [Hospital]. One of the young house staff lived round the corner from us, and he would always call up about two days before and say, 'Mrs. Cope, may I go and get the turkeys?' Everybody knew that I got the turkeys from the Window Shop. Once Alice Broch said, 'Would you mind please not talking about the turkeys quite so much? We can't cook everybody's turkey!'"

Alice Cope

"We are having great difficulty to attract young people for steady jobs. While our aging work force tends to look toward retirement, a pension plan, insurance, sickness benefits mean a lot. Younger people are more interested in current benefits—high pay, free weekends, flexible schedules, overtime, and holiday pay. There is basically very little interest in restaurant work as young people do not care for evening work—many take classes, have full-time morning jobs. Students are still available. They need a lot of training and supervision and as so many of our old workers are gone or will leave us in the near future, the outlook is not encouraging.

"Our profits are low and the curve is still downward as labor costs will continue to increase. (Five cents more per hour for waitresses since Sept. 1st).

Report to board by Alice Broch, 1963

"The trouble with me is that I am sixty-five years old. My husband will lose his job in March '64 or maybe earlier. He is not feeling very well, and I have to think of retirement, get ready for it. This is a most painful thing to do. I hate the thought of it, but I am forced to face it...."

Alice Broch

"When Mrs. Broch told employees and the board in mid-October 1963 that she wished to retire, each of us was dismayed. We were right, for no matter how hard everyone tried, nothing was ever the same again in the Restaurant and Bakery. We have missed her for thirty-five years in Cambridge and know how lucky we were to have been part of her life.

"She has always reminded me of that part of the ninety-first Psalm where David sings, 'He shall cover thee with his feathers, and under his wings shalt thou trust.' Feathers seem exactly right for Alice Perutz Broch—warm, light, comforting, and encompassing.

Dorothy Dahl upon Mrs. Broch's death

Ilse Heyman

Ilse Heyman is petite, attractive, and soft spoken. She is always impeccably dressed, reflecting perhaps the exquisite taste that symbolized the Window Shop for three decades. Even more remarkable are her quiet inner strength and the courage and resilience she summoned to survive World War II.

After her entire family was deported from Nazi-occupied Holland in 1943 (they had emigrated to Amsterdam in 1933 when Hitler came to power), Ilse was sent to a slave labor camp in Holland, where she assembled radio tubes for German airplanes. The operation was run by Philips, the Dutch electronics company, to save their many Jewish employees. She and her group of young women, seventeen to twenty-one years old, were sent to Auschwitz briefly when the Allied invasion of Europe was imminent and escaped death by being moved throughout Germany to work. Toward the end of the war, after being marched and transported by cattle car from camp to camp in a bitterly cold winter, Ilse's small group was exchanged for German prisoners of war and taken to Sweden by the Red Cross. Her parents, brother, and grandmother all died in the Holocaust.

After a year in Sweden, Ilse emigrated to Brookline, Massachusetts, where her uncle lived, in March 1946. She was twenty-three years old and very apprehensive about life in the United States and finding a job to support herself; she wondered whether she would be comfortable living with her American family. Her fears were short-lived: she and her younger cousin, a high school student and "an overprotected only child," bonded immediately and became close friends. Her English improved, and she found work in a small garment factory in Boston. There she encountered blatant anti-Semitism when one of her coworkers, angry at her Jewish boss, blurted out that she did not blame Hitler for what he did to the Jews. "I realized I had to get out," Ilse said.

She had heard of the Window Shop because her aunt had knitted little baby garments for sale there. Fortuitously, Lore Kadden, a family friend who had worked at the Window Shop, said, "You must come to Cambridge and meet Mary Mohrer." Ilse did and "was immediately charmed by the whole Window Shop setting, a small room, and everything was in good taste," she said in an interview in 2004. She hoped she could do alterations, but business was slow in the Gift and Dress Shop. A month later, however, Mary Mohrer's assistant left, and Ilse was hired in March 1947. She would remain at the Window Shop until it closed, and Mary would become not only her coworker and mentor, but her close friend and neighbor.

Scared stiff and shy and lacking self-confidence as she began her job, Ilse said she struggled to learn the basics of the retail business. The shop's move to Brattle Street was under way, and Mary Mohrer was often away, working with the architect. Fortunately, the bookkeeper worked nearby and helped introduce Ilse to the world of sales—and how to tell the difference between a charge and cash sale.

Despite the difficult beginnings, Ilse "worked her tail off," she liked the work and became more comfortable with the customers. But perhaps the most important benefit of the Window Shop was the friendships she made there. Coworkers and customers alike became friends of the young Holocaust survivor, and many of those friendships deepened after the Window Shop closed. Tamar Wurmfeld, who started as a baker and then a waitress for the Restaurant, had helped out in the Gift and Dress Shop as an occasional packer. At a busy time when sales help was needed, "Mary said, 'Call Tamar,' and Tamar threw off her apron and sold her first coat. She became a very wonderful coworker, who always invited me for Jewish holidays," said Ilse. Tamar and Ilse remain close friends.

"One young couple came in, and I liked them immediately," Ilse recalled. "She bought a white Dutch teapot, and we started to talk. Her husband was a drama professor, and she taught nursery school. When they had their first child, I was their first babysitter, and when I injured my foot, I lived with them for ten days until I could go back to work. It was a lovely friendship," and one that has endured through several moves and over many miles.

Board members, too, became more than just associates working with the staff on a beloved enterprise. Alice Cope, a longtime board member and president from 1948 to 1954, "always noticed everything," Ilse said. Shortly after Ilse's arrival at the shop, Alice Cope said, "Ilse, don't you think it's time for you to see one of our psychiatrists?" (The Viennese Analytic Society came to the Window Shop every Saturday afternoon for coffee and cake.) Ilse was not ready then, but after thinking about it, she decided to get some help. The psychiatrist recognized that she was in delayed mourning and worked with her for a year.

Dr. Oliver Cope also became a trusted friend, as well as the physician who cared for all the health problems of the Window Shop employees—and they were considerable. One evening around Christmas, Ilse's longtime hernia flared up. Dr. Cope went to her apartment and personally took her to Massachusetts General Hospital. "He wheeled me in," said Ilse with a smile, "and I don't think too many patients are wheeled in by their surgeon!"

Ilse Heyman's friendship with Mary Mohrer was complicated. As gifted and warm as Mary was, she could be prickly and domineering. Ilse said, "I had never been able to rebel against my parents. We were immigrants [in Holland], my mother wasn't well, and my father had a hard time keeping us afloat, so I grew up doing what was expected of me. But with Mary, I had to stand on my own feet and become independent. It was very difficult with someone like Mary, who, however much she loved me, also wanted to have me totally in her life and control me."

The two women lived next door to one another in an apartment house near Harvard Square. They walked to and from work together, talking all the way. "At night," said Ilse, "we would never go to sleep without calling each other." When Mary's health began to fail, it was Ilse who took care of her until her death in 1995. Mary Mohrer's influence on Ilse's life is inestimable, and even today her name enters most conversations about the Window Shop.

Amid the joy of working at the Window Shop and developing a circle of close, supportive friends came the stunning blow that after thirty-three years, the shop would close its doors. Bitterness over the board's treatment of the employees darkens Ilse's memories of the shop's final chapter. "Around July 1972, it seems that they [the board] decided to close the Window Shop. They did not tell any of us. Mary went to England on a buying trip. Nothing was said." Mary returned with some "treasures" for the Gift Shop as she always did. The board informed her that the shop would close by the end of the year, and that she should not speak about it to anyone. Furthermore, she had to cancel all her orders. "This was devastating to Mary. She felt she would lose her integrity," said Ilse. "The board practically wrote her letters for her. It was absolutely awful."

Fighting the depression that comes with such a significant loss, Ilse Heyman found a job at the Women's Educational and Industrial Union, in the needlepoint shop, and was able to apply some of the business practices she learned at the

Window Shop to her new employment. She told of the time Mary Mohrer came to visit, and the manager of the shop said, "Ah, thank you for sending us your wonderful Ilse." To which Ilse replied, "Well, I'm wonderful because Mary taught me." She added, "I got my self-confidence at the Window Shop."

After retiring from the Women's Union, she was a volunteer in the Cambridge School system for fifteen years, and she has told her personal history to fifth- and sixth-graders at the Cambridgeport (Massachusetts) School. On May 11, 2005, Ilse Heyman was the principal speaker at the annual Holocaust Commemoration in Cambridge. More than two hundred people heard her harrowing story of Holocaust survival. She concluded her talk with these words: "As Philips had saved me from death at Auschwitz, so the Window Shop helped me (and many others) to become part of a community and lead a life." The entire audience stood and applauded, with respect and gratitude.

On November 1, 2005, she received a Peace and Justice Award from the City of Cambridge.

Elisabeth Martens

Interviewed in 2003 at her home in Springfield, Massachusetts, Elisabeth Martens at ninety-three is still a commanding figure. She is tall and erect, with a pleasant face that suggests a young woman of beauty. Although she suffers from failing eyesight and less than vivid memories of the long-ago Window Shop, she leaves no doubt about its importance in her life.

"We all got along very, very well together. We really had a sense of togetherness, that we were all in the same boat," Mrs. Martens said. She added with a smile, "We were one big family."

Mrs. Martens and her husband, who had been a judge in Germany when they fled Hitler with their two children, found themselves in Orange, Massachusetts, in 1942. Mr. Martens had an administrative job in a paper mill there, but the small town of four thousand people didn't suit the Martenses. "We came from Hamburg, Germany, a city the size of Boston, and we weren't very happy in Orange. Some people thought we had personal correspondence with Hitler, and some people were very nice." Friends helped them relocate to Cambridge, where Mrs. Martens found her way to the Window Shop, while her husband eventually found work in a bank. Their children were ten and seven years old at the time, and Mrs. Martens's mother-in-law, who also emigrated from Germany, could care for them.

Mrs. Martens started working at 102 Mount Auburn Street, "cleaning toilets and doing whatever needed to be done." After the move to Brattle Street in 1947, she became a waitress in the Restaurant and then a supervisor. "I trained about twenty-five college girls every summer, and we didn't allow nonsense!" Training included instruction in how to approach customers, how to serve the food, how to dress nicely (hairnets were required), and above all, politeness was stressed. She points out that the "basic crew" was all Europeans from Austria, Germany, and Hungary.

Mrs. Martens shared supervisory duties with Mrs. Benfey, and she explains that each of them worked long, sometimes overlapping, hours. Their days often ended at eight or nine o'clock at night. During the busiest times, the women pitched in wherever they were needed to help the waitresses and kitchen staff.

Mrs. Martens greatly admired Alice Broch, the legendary manager of the Restaurant, and the two women maintained their friendship after Mrs. Broch retired in 1964.

After Mrs. Broch's retirement, the Restaurant "wasn't the same any more. We got new managers, but they were different; they did what they wanted, and they weren't there all the time." Mrs. Martens admits to being upset about the new managers, who didn't seem to take their jobs as seriously as Mrs. Broch had done.

Nonetheless, she remembers the good times, the fun the staff had, and the frequent laughter. For example, a customer asked Hertha Becher, the elderly woman at the Bakery counter, what a *Dobos torte* was. The reply, delivered sternly, was, "A *Dobos torte* is a *Dobos torte*!"

Unhappy with the post-Broch regime at the Window Shop, Mrs. Martens left in 1967, after twenty-five years in the Restaurant. Her coworker, Mrs. Benfey, had left three years earlier. Mrs. Martens, then only fifty-eight, worked as a statistician at McLean Hospital in Belmont, Massachusetts, and remained in that position for seventeen years until she retired.

Doris Martin

A slim, attractive blonde, Doris Martin was interviewed in March 2003 at 56 Brattle Street, former home of the Window Shop. She was a war bride from Germany and arrived in the Boston area in February 1952, with her small son. Her husband had preceded her.

"Some friends of mine thought I was terribly, terribly homesick," Doris recalled. "They knew about the Window Shop and that some German people were working there and suggested it would be a good place for me." She started working as a bus girl in April 1952, moved up to becoming a waitress, and then began helping out in the Bakery as time allowed, because her son was in kindergarten. Her husband became ill, and she needed to work longer hours in the Bakery. "At the time, Mrs. Broch made it possible for me to work in several departments by sending my son to camp, paid for by the Window Shop," she said.

Doris Martin began working full-time in the Bakery. Mrs. Broch hired a French baker, Henry C. Lelaurain, to teach her to become a professional baker, using recipes from Mrs. Broch's well-thumbed cookbook. Doris then became head baker and supervisor of the Window Shop Bakery.

Mrs. Broch became a very good friend and Doris stayed in touch with her after her retirement. She would send Mrs. Broch copies of the order forms from the Bakery. "When I started there," recalled Doris, "they made about seven *Linzer* trees [*Linzer tortes* in the shape of a Christmas tree] at Christmastime. Later we were making about three hundred or four hundred to mail all over the country, and it made her very happy to see how we had expanded."

Doris Martin worked very hard. She was the first one in the Bakery at 4:30 AM and often worked until six or seven o'clock in the evening. There were three bakers and some part-time people who came in to make cookies. Before Christmas, a night shift was hired, and the staff worked seven or fourteen days straight without a day off. "The only good thing was I enjoyed what I was doing, and I had a certain pride in it, especially when the Window Shop was sold and the [Cambridge Center for Adult Education] kept the Bakery, and I was asked to continue with it."

Doris is credited with building up the Bakery's wedding cake business. She adapted many of her cake recipes, added white frosting, and the results were enormously successful. Her friend and coworker Pearl Morrison said, "A particular kind of cake, like the Emperor Torte or the Hazelnut Cake or the Mocha Cake, people wanted those in a wedding cake and I constantly had to say, 'Doris, can you do this? Can you do that?' I pushed Doris to the wall!" For two or three years the Bakery participated in the wedding cake show at the Park Plaza Hotel in

Boston, and it also held special invitation-only shows at the Window Shop. Doris would make several different cakes, and brides-to-be could sample them before ordering.

Establishing a price for some of these specialty items was a challenge. Doris would figure out the ingredients, add in the labor, and come up with a price. "Oh my God, Pearl, that's very high!" she would protest, but the customer would never complain—which undoubtedly meant that the Bakery was undercharging.

Asked which cakes and tortes were the most popular, Doris answered, "The Mozart [cake] and *Sacher torte*. The coffee cakes were very popular, and of course the brioche was the best seller of all. And people went crazy over the cookies … oh, and the rum balls!"

Today Doris Martin lives in Brighton, Massachusetts. She still bakes, often using Mrs. Broch's recipes, although she is more likely to bake one cake instead of ten at a time. Some of these recipes appear in the Appendix.

Mary Mohrer

Mary Mohrer *was* the Window Shop. She was there at the beginning and the end; thirty-three years of her life were dedicated to the organization and, most important, to the refugees who sought haven here. Mary (and everyone called her "Mary") used her multi-faceted talents to run an innovative and successful retail shop, and to help her fellow refugees find jobs, housing, and even new careers.

When Mary arrived in Cambridge, she was a bright, vivacious young woman with a warm personality, and a flair for clothes and design. She was the quintessential "people person" and knew that she had a gift for connecting with all sorts of people. In the early days of the Window Shop, she knew the refugees' despair, turmoil, and challenges, since she was also a refugee.

Mary was raised in Vienna, studied fine arts, and spoke five languages. She escaped Nazi persecution after the Anschluss in 1938 by emigrating to Switzerland. "I arrived in New York at the end of 1938 after an odyssey through the world," she said in a 1984 oral history interview.[67] She lived in New York briefly, doing small translation jobs, but decided not to stay. "I really wanted to go to Seattle [where] at least I would have the mountains and the scenery I loved so much. But the trip was terribly expensive, and the night bus to Cambridge cost $3.50." Cambridge appealed to her because it was a university town. She stayed with a distant cousin who had provided her with an affidavit and then took a room in Cambridge in exchange for taking care of an "obstreperous eight-year-old boy."

The Boston Refugee Committee introduced her to "a group of Cambridge women—they are all non-Jewish" who had just started a thrift shop in Harvard

Square for the benefit of newly arrived refugees. The Cambridge women found they needed an interpreter and asked this petite, blue-eyed young woman to help. Mary was job-hunting but volunteered to interpret in her spare time. As she spent more time (unpaid!) at 37 Church Street, Mary's retailing intuition led her to suggest to the founders that the refugees themselves make items to sell at the newly named Window Shop.

"They brought some hats and scarves to sell. That was all we had," she recalled. "And so people came." And so the Window Shop was on its way, changing and evolving according to the needs of those who sought its help.

She was offered $12 a week, but in reality she was paid only $7, since there was never enough money, and the consignment workers had to be paid first. She once said, "When there was money, I had frankfurts and beans for lunch. When there was no money, no frankfurts—maybe no beans."

By early spring of 1939, refugees brought more products to sell: handkerchief umbrellas, bakery goods, and leather flowers, and some offered dressmaking services. Soon enough, "it started to really be a social agency," Mary recalled, and she was the one person who could listen to the refugees' problems, many of which were psychological.

Having outgrown the small Church Street venue, the Window Shop moved to 102 Mount Auburn Street in September 1939. "We had no mover," said Mary Mohrer. "We moved everything, every board, ourselves." At the Window Shop's new home, Mary could flex her design muscles by creating a beautiful sales area for items that were still being produced by refugees. While Mary had innate talents and flawless intuition, she lacked business training, but fortunately a board member, Bessie Jones, took her under her wing and taught her sound business practices. Under Mrs. Jones's stewardship, the Dress Shop was established following the "dirndl episode," and it soon became Mary Mohrer's "baby." She became the full-time manager of the Gift and Dress Shop in 1942, still at the rather miserly salary of $12 a week.

It was on Brattle Street that the Window Shop flourished. The move to renovated space allowed Mary Mohrer to achieve her greatest success. The shop was tastefully decorated and stocked with glassware, pottery, casserole dishes, wooden bowls, fabrics, and women's clothing—all personally selected by Mary. With the blessing of the Window Shop board, she began to go abroad in search of foreign products. "I was very interested in crafts," she said, "and I had a good feeling about what this country could use and couldn't use." One of her early trips to Scandinavia included a visit to Finland, where she bought some "marvelous weavings," to Denmark for stainless steel ware and pottery, and to Copenhagen for specialty items at Den Permanente, its landmark store. In Finland, Mary declined Marimekko fabrics, finding them "too heavy" for American tastes—of course,

Marimekko was later imported by rival Design Research in Cambridge and proved very popular with customers. Nonetheless, Mary Mohrer's international merchandise gave the Window Shop a tremendous boost, not only financially because the "markup on these things was very great, but also it was a prestige thing. And once it had started, things kept coming."

Across the courtyard, the Window Shop Restaurant and Bakery was beginning to thrive under the leadership of Mary's counterpart, the legendary Alice Broch. Customers who came for coffee and pastry or for lunch would stop at the Gift and Dress Shop to see what Mary had brought back from her buying trips around the world. In ten years, Mary Mohrer's Gift and Dress Shop had built a loyal customer base among the affluent, influential, and discerning residents of Cambridge and Greater Boston and was enjoying financial success.

But the needs of the refugee employees for social services continued unabated, and although volunteer social workers were now available to the refugees, Mary continued to operate her own social services network. Her oral histories are replete with stories of immigrant families in desperate straits whom she helped and who stayed in touch with her for many years.

Twenty years after its thrift-shop beginnings, the Window Shop was still prospering and had become a Harvard Square landmark. In April 1959, a board member summed up twenty years of success:

> The Gift and Dress Shop has changed with the times and today sells clothes bought in New York and gifts imported by Miss Mohrer on her trips to Europe. But some of the top dress designers were helped by the Shop in their early days in America. Miss Mohrer's greatest pleasure is discovering talented young people who design beautiful jewelry, silver, or ceramics, and starting them on their way to success.[68]

But hard times lay just ahead. As chronicled in Chapter 3, the Window Shop's fortunes began a slow, painful downward spiral in the mid-sixties. While the Gift and Dress Shop continued to post profits much of the time, those profits were dedicated to supporting the failing Restaurant and Bakery—causing continuing friction between the two departments. Mary Mohrer's greatest challenge came in March 1965, when the board asked her to become general manager of the entire operation. Her five-year tenure was fraught with the problems generated by the Restaurant and Bakery that are outlined in Chapter 3. The malaise affected sales in the Gift and Dress Shop, and in late 1970, exhausted and discouraged, Mary resigned her dual position and returned, "with great relief," to running the Gift and Dress Shop in hopes of restoring it to profitability.

Two years later, the board decided to close the Window Shop and to continue as a foundation to provide scholarships and aid to the deserving and needy. The employees were heartsick at the news, none more so than the shop's longest-serving one. "I'll be sixty-three on the day of closing," Mary told writer Ellen Goodman.[69] "I never thought about my age before, but when they said we were closing, I thought, 'Well, now I'm old.' After thirty-three years, you say good-bye to your friends and close the door. I don't even know where the keys are."

In fact, on that awful day, Ilse Heyman recalls that, "Mary locked herself in the bathroom and would not come out. Finally, Dr. Oliver Cope got her out and managed to take her out the back door."

She worked for a year in the gift shop at Massachusetts General Hospital, where she had to stand on her feet all day. After retiring, Mary continued to do what she did best—working with people in a number of different capacities. She counseled high school students at Cambridge Rindge and Latin School near her home, was a charter member of the Institute of Learning in Retirement at Harvard, and occasionally taught French there.

After her death in 1995, Cambridge Rindge and Latin High School established a peer counseling program in her name.

For thirty-three years, Mary Mohrer gave her all to the Window Shop and ended up with a broken heart. There are, however, still legions of former employees, board members, artists, artisans, and craftspeople who remember and respect her. In coming to America, Mary Mohrer could have chosen any number of professions. Fate chose her to lead the Window Shop and to influence all those whose lives she touched.

Olga Schiffer

In three short years at the Window Shop, from 1939 to 1942, Olga Schiffer, in partnership with Alice Perutz Broch, launched the Tea Room that soon evolved into the Restaurant. Mrs. Schiffer exemplifies the refugee women of her time: the wife of a successful lawyer, mother of two children, who found herself the bread-winner for her family when her husband reentered law school. Her story is told by her daughter Eva Schiffer, a retired professor of Germanic Languages at the University of Massachusetts at Amherst, in her booklet, *Sketches*, published in 1995. Excerpts are quoted here with the author's permission.

Olga Grunberger Schiffer was born in 1895 in Moravia. She grew up in impe-rial Vienna, attended formal balls and (standing room only) the Vienna Opera. She was a rock climber and led her children up Alpine trails. Her happiest child-hood memories were of the family farm in Moravia.

She and her attorney husband Ludwig, with their children Eva and George, lived a very comfortable life in a six-room apartment in Vienna until the *Anschluss*, the annexation of Austria by the Nazis, on March 12, 1938. The Schiffer children were sent to stay with family friends in Groningen, Holland, while their parents returned to Vienna, where Ludwig Schiffer planned to resume his legal work.

"My father was arrested about two weeks [later]," writes Eva Schiffer. "There was no formal charge—none was needed: he was a highly successful Jewish defense attorney with a great many clients, many of them no doubt Jewish. He spent the next six months in the concentration camps of Dachau and Buchenwald.

"My mother sprang into action. Like Jews throughout Nazi Germany, she applied for immigration visas to the embassy or consulate of every country in the world whose borders were still open.… With persistent frequency, ignoring her own danger, she made inquiries of the Gestapo about my father's whereabouts and status as a detainee. She secured every last possible document required to clear the way for permission for him to leave the country the moment he was released. She took a course in Swedish massage and learned to make intricately knotted and colorful string belts. She invented business that supposedly required his signature and succeeded in having it supplied to her—thus reassuring her each time that he was still alive. And most incredibly of all, she obtained permission one day to visit him in Dachau."

Amazingly, Schiffer was released just after *Kristallnacht* (November 9, 1938), and the Schiffer parents joined their children in Holland. In Rotterdam, he immediately applied for visas for the family to leave for America. In due course, an affidavit was secured, provided by an American couple who pledged that they would be financially responsible for the Schiffers, and visas were issued for the family. They set sail from Southampton and landed in New York on September 13, 1939.

"Our family had $500 when we landed in New York," writes Eva Schiffer. Her parents were allowed to take their belongings out of Vienna, but no more money. "Among the luggage my parents brought to Groningen with them were two large and heavy suitcases full of textile samples: while my mother was coming to America prepared to do Swedish massage and sell homemade string belts, my father had allowed a former client and textile exporter to persuade him that he could turn himself into a salesman. During the four weeks we spent in New York, my father went door to door with his suitcases, sometimes accompanied by me.… Finally he decided that this was hopeless and nonsensical: a lawyer was all that he knew how to be, and there had to be a way for him back to the profession he loved. The American legal system, being fundamentally different from the

European, this meant studying law all over again at age 43. Somehow he was referred to a Mr. Richard Hale, a wealthy partner in a prestigious Boston law firm, who advised him how to apply to Harvard; and soon we were on our way to Cambridge, Massachusetts.... My father had his hands full with improving his English and competing with students more than twenty years younger than he, as he worked his way into an unfamiliar approach to the practice of law.

"Meanwhile, one small problem remained to be solved: what were we to live on? Occasional opportunities arose for my father to earn small amounts of money with translations. Once he helped a refugee woman, Mary Mohrer, to document a claim and accepted in lieu of payment—it was all she was able to offer—her complete blue-onion (*Zwiebelmuster*) set of dinnerware: adequate payment in value, I am sure, as well as, probably for her, a wrenching sacrifice, but not much help with paying our rent."

Olga Schiffer found the Window Shop on Church Street which, in October 1939, was a thrift shop for the benefit of refugees. "My mother tried her luck with her string belts, and struck up an acquaintance with another Viennese woman, Alice ("Liesl") Perutz. Soon the two of them decided to try running something like a Viennese *Kaffeehaus*. Both came from comfortable Viennese households and were used to having cooks and other servants; I don't think either of them had done much baking or cooking in her life. But they put together their mothers' cookbooks and started out.

"For a while they made *Apfelstrudl* and *Linzer torte* and *Malakov torte* and *Vanillekipferl* and *petits fours* ... and who knows what else of the innumerable high-calorie, high-in-cholesterol delicacies of my childhood, all, needless to say, 'from scratch' and with no shortcuts. To give the place some European ambiance, they wore the dirndls they had brought from Europe.

"Of course there was good, real, strong coffee, with and without *Schlag* (whipped cream). Room was made in the store for a few tables. The two women did all the serving. It was at first a tea-time operation. They baked at home. Harvard wives endowed with cars made the deliveries.

"Eventually my mother and Liesl Perutz decided to try cooking evening meals. Out came the recipes: *Wiener Schnitzel, Goulasch, Rahmschnitzel, Paprikahuhn....* Success was instantaneous."

The Schiffers then settled into their new lives in Cambridge; Eva attended Cambridge Rindge and Latin School, and her younger brother George entered Brown and Nichols, a private day school in Cambridge, "on a scholarship no doubt obtained with the help of one of the good Harvard faculty wives," writes Eva Schiffer.

Ludwig Schiffer had hoped to find employment with a Boston law firm after graduating from Harvard Law School in 1942. His mentor Mr. Hale made it very plain that this was "an unrealistic hope for a Jew, even a highly qualified Jew.... So my father explored New York and found a position with a large law firm, and my parents moved to Kew Gardens in Queens where they had managed to find an apartment in a complex which did not bear, as many did, a plaque permanently mounted on the brick façade that read: 'Negroes and Jews need not apply.'

"Four years later, he left the firm and established his own small and perennially struggling law practice.... I was studying for my M.A. at Radcliffe when Dad made the decision to strike out on his own, and I managed to get scholarship aid, and employment at the Window Shop, to replace the financial support he could no longer provide. My mother supplemented their income by a succession of jobs—I remember one in a factory that manufactured costume jewelry—before becoming Dad's secretary."

Ludwig Schiffer died in 1961. Olga Schiffer then moved to Amherst, Massachusetts, to live with her daughter. She died in 1984.

Tamar Wurmfeld

Between them, Tamar and Henry Wurmfeld accumulated many years of Window Shop wisdom and experience. Mrs. Wurmfeld started baking for the Window Shop, became a waitress, and ultimately was a salesperson in the Gift and Dress Shop. Mr. Wurmfeld, a chef, was "discovered" one summer working in a Cape Cod hotel by Mrs. Broch, who was impressed with his culinary abilities and offered him a position at the Window Shop. Tamar Wurmfeld had emigrated from Germany to Palestine, where she met her husband. In 1952, the Wurmfelds moved to New York, before arriving in Cambridge in October 1953. They had four-year-old twin girls and the family rented the tiny Window Shop-owned apartment at 5 Story Street. Before their furniture arrived from New York, Lotte Benfey, the Restaurant supervisor, invited them to stay with her. "We had never met the woman," said Tamar. "She was just wonderful. This was the way people were."

While Henry cooked in the Restaurant, Tamar's employment at the Window Shop began one busy Christmas season when she was asked if she baked. "Sure," I said. "I needed to make some money, so they brought me pots of dough and jam for the *Linzer torte*. And while the kids were playing, I sat there and rolled the *Linzer torte*!" Not long after, she was asked, probably by Mrs. Broch, to work as a waitress while the children were in school. She learned how from another German waitress, Ursula Loewy.

Tamar Wurmfeld, daughter of a rabbi, was a trained nurse. She is an extremely likeable woman who exudes warmth and loves to laugh. She also has a take-charge air about her without needing to be in control. She is intelligent, keenly interested in the world, and clear-eyed about what the Window Shop was—and was not. She now lives in a sunny apartment in Belmont, Massachusetts, and leads an active life. Her husband Henry died several years ago.

The next busy Christmas season, Mary Mohrer asked Tamar if she could help with packing gifts to be mailed. Her hours would coincide with her children's time in kindergarten—in fact, she could make her own hours. Tamar agreed, and, ever versatile, she was recruited to help sell a coat to a customer when the Dress Shop staff was suddenly short-handed. Tamar said, "I hadn't the slightest notion about selling and certainly not selling fashion. I wasn't brought up to like that." To her amazement, the sale was made, and thus began her career in the Gift and Dress Shop.

Asked about her interactions with board members, Tamar responds enthusiastically about some of the larger-than-life women who shaped and helped run the Window Shop, especially Lillian Cohan, who "was so full of life. She could sell you a dead mouse, and you would go out thinking that you had come in for that dead mouse!" Having worked on both sides of the Window Shop, Tamar is well qualified to criticize the decisions made by the board that led to the closing of the shop. The decision to hire Mary Mohrer to run both the Gift Shop and the Restaurant was misguided and destined to fail. "There was nobody there who could have done it, but perhaps if it had been temporary.... It was very difficult for Mary, and she ended up being hurt." Tamar pointed out that the Restaurant was in trouble before Mary Mohrer took over, and the parade of managers and consultants who followed Alice Broch appeared never to understand the culture of the Window Shop. "The Window Shop was a great haven of security for all the immigrants," said Tamar. "You didn't get fired just because somebody else came along." Employees stayed in their jobs for a long time; there were even some waitresses who were close to eighty years old, and they were assigned a bus girl or bus-boy who could help carry the heavy trays up the stairs.

After the Window Shop closed in December 1972, Tamar worked at Massachusetts General Hospital and contrasted the feeling of job insecurity there with the security offered by the Window Shop—at least until it all ended. Summarizing her Window Shop experience, Tamar was philosophical: "The fact that you felt safe was wonderful. They were wonderful years. I'm glad I was there. I'm sorry it's gone, but this is real life."

Portraits

The Window Shop Board

The Window Shop Board, 1941. From left on bench, Margaret Blumgart, Alice Cope, Sally Wolfinsohn, Mrs. Sandorf, F. Frank Vorenberg, Margaret Smith, Charles Dunbar, Frances Fremont-Smith, Helen Eisemann, Elizabeth Malone.

The Men of the Window Shop

The Window Shop was shaped, guided, and run by women. During a time when women were not as prevalent in the work force as they are today, at the shop men took a back seat but were often called upon for financial and legal advice. In the history of the shop, there was only one male president. It should be noted that husbands of board members were largely supportive, but, with a few exceptions, remained invisible.

It is interesting to note that many of the men were influential board members at the beginning—during incorporation in 1941—and at the end, in the fall of 1972 when arrangements for the sale of the property were made. In both periods, the women of the board felt that professional male expertise was needed for the myriad legal affairs and business transactions. Among the incorporators were Charles F. Dunbar, an attorney; William Ehrlich, treasurer; and F. Frank Vorenberg, president of Gilchrist's, a major Boston department store. Present at the demise of the Window Shop were Richard Kahan, board president from 1972 to 1974, and James Heskett, both of Harvard Business School. Also influential in helping the shop develop its personnel practices was Alvah Kindall, personnel director at Filene's department store,

Reuben Lurie, an attorney and later a judge, often served as "the voice of reason" on the board. He once reminded his colleagues on the board that "the Window Shop is never in the red because of what we are doing. We should not confuse the red figure with the black figure of accomplishment."[70] Equally important was the expertise he shared with the employees. An anonymous Window Shop refugee wrote: "Reuben Lurie made himself available to all our group who came to him with their problems. This was invaluable to a group new to this country and its ways. They were displaced persons in more than name, truly in need of the advice he was so willing to give."

Dr. Oliver Cope, husband of Board President Alice Cope and brother of Board President Elizabeth Aub, shared his wife's concern for and devotion to the refugees. It was a joint visit to Germany in the early 1930s that alerted the Copes to conditions there and made them eager to help the refugees who could escape from the Nazis. Dr. Cope was instrumental in referring employees to the best medical specialists in the area, and he made a vast difference in the lives of many on whom he lavished his friendship and medical expertise. Dr. Oliver Cope died one day after his wife, on May 2, 1994.

Perhaps the most influential and longest-serving board member was Walter Bieringer, a Boston businessman, national authority on immigration, and "guiding light in helping European Jews resettle in the U.S.," according to the *Boston Globe*. A profile of this extraordinary man appears later in this chapter.

Fred Alexander, for many years the Window Shop's accountant, was a German refugee, who watched over the shop's often-precarious budgets and guided the board's financial decisions. His profile also appears in this chapter.

Other notable men who served on the Window Shop Board of Directors were attorneys John Ferry and Hans Loeser and businessman Hans Kroto.

Fred Alexander

The following biography of Fred Alexander was written by his sons, Jack and Robert Alexander, for this book:

Fred Alexander was born in Hamburg, Germany, in 1912. As a young man he was very athletic, boxing in the Bar Kochba Club and skiing with the famous Hannes Schneider Ski Team. He followed his father into the banking profession. In 1936 he married Ruth Becher and they had a son, Jack.

With Hitler's rise to power, their life changed. Fred helped Jews leave Germany for Palestine, and in 1939 he sent Ruth, her mother, Hertha Becher, and Jack to England. Several weeks later he joined them. After a year in England, the family moved to Boston, where, with the help of IMAS (Immigrants' Mutual Aid Society), Fred found a job as an unskilled laborer in a leather factory. He studied at Bentley College in Waltham, Massachusetts, at night to become an accountant, joined what was then the only Jewish accounting firm in Boston, and eventually became a CPA with his own firm. Friends and clients grew to respect Fred's commitment to ethical business practices. As an example, he never broke confidences.

Both he and Ruth loved their new country and especially Boston, with its culture and diverse population. They had a second son, Robert, and established themselves in their own home in Belmont.

Throughout their lives, Fred and Ruth enjoyed helping others overcome hardships and experience success. The Window Shop, where Fred audited the books and sat *ex officio* on the board, provided ample opportunity to apply these values. As long as the shop lasted, it was a focus of the Alexanders' lives. Hertha Becher worked at the Restaurant counter as "Mrs. Sunshine," and almost every weekend Ilse Heyman, Mary Mohrer, and others from the shop arrived at the Alexanders' home for Sunday dinner. Afterward, everyone napped, awoke for coffee at 3:00 PM, and then left to prepare for the work week. Alexander celebrations always included a large contingent of Window Shop regulars.

As competitors arose to lure customers from the Window Shop, Fred worked with the staff to save it. But he was unsuccessful, and the board voted to close the shop.

Fred had firm ideas of what was important and what was not; he had an independent and judicious mind, a considerate soul, and a warm humor that endeared him to many.

Elizabeth Aub

Mrs. Aub (front), Eleanor Roosevelt, and Alice Broch.

Mrs. Aub was a talented woman whose contributions to the Window Shop over a thirty-five-year span are vast. She was a trained architect, married to an eminent Boston physician, mother of three daughters, and a good friend to all at the Window Shop. She was the sister-in-law of Alice Cope, longtime board member and Window Shop president from 1948 to 1954.

A 1977 obituary in the *Boston Globe* described Mrs. Aub as "a shy woman of keen intelligence and quiet personal charm and grace. [She was] an accomplished musician, her favorite instrument being the cello." She was a graduate of Bryn

Mawr College and received her architectural degree from MIT. Her daughter, Nancy Aub Gleason, said, "She never worked for money. She designed our house, she designed a dormitory at the Cambridge School, she did some architectural models. I asked her when she was getting on whether she was disappointed that she had never made a career as an architect. She didn't know what I was talking about. It was just another era. Daddy was very successful, she didn't need to worry about the money, and she was an incredible volunteer."

Mrs. Aub's architectural skills were noticed by the Window Shop Board. She was elected to the board in May 1942 and then was promptly asked to oversee some construction work being done to the shop, which was at that time at 102 Mount Auburn Street. She was soon elected treasurer in October 1942, "a position which she graced for eleven and a half years and which she always said was her favorite," according to Board Member Sally Wolfinsohn.

"I'm not aware of my mother having had any connection with refugees before this," said Nancy Aub Gleason. "My father was Jewish; my mother was a Quaker. She would have been, I'm sure, very alarmed at what was going on in Europe. Her social conscience would have been aroused, but I suspect that Aunt Alice [Cope] was involved first [in the Window Shop] and got Mother involved. Mother was very good at math, and it was sort of logical for her to become treasurer. Then the architectural side of it came up and the human side."

Her major architectural contribution came during the transformation in 1946 of the Cock Horse on Brattle Street into the Window Shop. Mrs. Aub was chairman of the building committee, with members Mary Mohrer and Alice Broch. As Mrs. Wolfinsohn noted, "She was at 56 Brattle Street for long hours and from basement to attic."

On the memorable day in May 1950 when Mrs. Roosevelt came for lunch, Window Shop President Alice Cope was in Europe, so Elizabeth Aub did the honors. "Excitement ran high and a bit of anxiety with it, but lunch was delicious. Mrs. Roosevelt was most gracious and the write-up next morning in 'My Day' was all that we had hoped for," reported Mrs. Wolfinsohn.

On April 1, 1954, Mrs. Aub became president of the Window Shop and remained in that position for an eventful ten years. Her friend and fellow board member Hedy Sturges recalls, "When I came on the board [in the early '50s], Elizabeth Aub was treasurer. When she became president, she wanted me to become the treasurer. I said, 'But Elizabeth, I don't know ...' She said, 'Hedy, money comes in and money goes out!'"

Under her leadership, the Window Shop adopted a pension plan and life insurance plan for employees, secured a wine license, completed major alterations in the Gift Shop and offices, enlarged and covered part of the courtyard, installed an alarm system and improved the air-conditioning system. At the end of her presidency, in 1965, she became the vice president for a year and then remained on the board until her death in 1977.

Her longtime friend and colleague Alice Broch summarized how much Mrs. Aub meant to the Window Shop community in a note dated Thanksgiving 1964, shortly after Mrs. Broch's retirement:

"You deserve much more gratitude and many more thanks than anyone can ever express. Not only for all the major contributions and your successful achievements, but for creating a firm ground under our feet by believing in the aims and purposes of the Shop so wholeheartedly. Your positive attitude has always been an inspiration to us, especially to E. M. [Elisabeth Martens] and L. B. [Lotte Benfey] and me. It was you who guided the flock, you took us by the hand and directed and helped us by sharing our problems with infinite patience. You gave us so much. How can anyone ever thank you adequately?"

Nancy Aub Gleason added that each year on her mother's birthday, until she died, the Window Shop "always gave her a birthday cake, and it was usually that mocha frosting with little red cherries on top, very delicately decorated. Gorgeous cake."

Marion Bever

Marion Bever was board president at a critical time. In fact, she presided over events leading to the traumatic final years of the Window Shop in 1972. Her association with the Window Shop began thirty years earlier, when she met the boats carrying refugees from Nazi-occupied countries. After the shop closed, Mrs. Bever was active on the scholarship committee, recruiting MIT and Harvard faculty wives as new board members who would become excellent interviewers of potential scholarship recipients. She was still there when the scholarship committee disbanded in 1987.

Marion Bever's mother, Mrs. Nathan Gordon, was an important figure in the Window Shop's early struggle for survival. A woman of means, she gave Alice Broch $300 and told her, "Go out and buy china for your tea shop." When Mrs. Gordon saw Mrs. Broch scrubbing the kitchen floor, she paid her own chauffeur to do the job nightly. She never indulged in unnecessary talk, and her generosity was coupled with immediate and appropriate action.

Mrs. Bever's contribution to the Window Shop was equally direct, generous, and appropriate. "She was central to the annual fundraising, making it a point to know anyone in the area that would have an interest," according to past President Dorothy Dahl. "Her knowledge of food was helpful in the Restaurant and Bakery, and her passion for style and design led her to deep interest in the Gift and Dress Shop." With Mary Mohrer and Hedy Sturges, she was instrumental in arranging fashion shows in the area to promote the Window Shop.

In the early, struggling days of the shop, Mrs. Bever was a waitress in the Restaurant, carrying heavy trays up and down the narrow stairway. She worked at the Bakery counter and weekly took out the trash with Margaret Earhart Smith.

Mrs. Bever died in December 1992. Her devotion to the Window Shop and its successor organization spanned fifty years.

Voices

"Marion was a wonderful person. She was my closest friend. I was with her when she died. Marion was a Bostonian, and she had many experiences. She was Jewish and felt discriminated against when she was young, but she was devoted to the Window Shop, as was her mother. Marion supported the Window Shop in every possible way. She was devoted to all the workers. She would have done anything for them."

Hedy Sturges

"Marion became secretary to the scholarship committee, producing monthly minutes so compelling and accurate that when they were read aloud at meetings, the room sometimes could not resist applauding. Few board members had her staying power, from meeting boats carrying refugees in the late 1930s to being a part of the disbandment decision for the scholarship committee in 1987."

Dorothy Dahl

Walter H. Bieringer[71]

The subhead in Walter Bieringer's obituary in the *Boston Globe* in 1990 reads, "Helped refugees resettle in America." That is succinct but a gross understatement. His active and influential role in assisting refugees made him a valuable and informed Window Shop board member from 1941 to 1970.

Mr. Bieringer was a very successful, Harvard-educated businessman in Boston, the executive vice president of Plymouth Rubber Company of Canton, Massachusetts. He was born in Boston in 1900 to Jewish parents who had emigrated to the United States from Germany as adolescents. In his own words, he was "not much involved with [his] Jewish background." He was the victim of anti-Semitism only once in his student days, when he was scheduled to receive a team letter as a member of the Harvard tennis team. It was not forthcoming, and a coach was overheard to remark that "Jews were ineligible for such a distinction." Yet, he subsequently explained, this incident did not leave a lasting impression because, "It was well known in these years that Harvard was anti-Semitic. Everyone just accepted this."

A January 1933 business trip to Germany and Austria was a major turning point in Mr. Bieringer's life. He experienced Nazi persecution of Jews firsthand, having been ordered off the sidewalk by some Nazis, and he described another incident: "In Vienna, a man jumped on the running board of my car and yelled, '*Jude raus*' (Jew, get out). That's what made me Jewish."[72] His role as an activist on behalf of Jews seeking to escape Nazi Germany, and later in assisting refugees in the Boston area, had begun. Upon his return to Boston, he founded the Boston Committee for Refugees, which consolidated several concerned community organizations of Protestant, Catholic, and Jewish members. The model was followed in other cities.

On his next business trip to Germany and Austria, he carried with him several American telephone directories from various parts of the country. When he met with groups of European Jews who wanted to immigrate to the United States, he asked individuals to look for the same name as theirs in the telephone books. When a match or even a near-match was found, Mr. Bieringer suggested they write to the American (he even brought sample letters in English and German) requesting an affidavit guaranteeing sponsorship. The Boston Committee had agreed to fund the cost of such affidavits. In many cases this scheme paved the way for victims of Nazi persecution to enter the United States.

Mr. Bieringer identified three stages in the immigration process: 1) rescue; 2) resettlement in the United States; and 3) adjustment to the new culture and environment. In addition to his attempts to rescue immigrants by means of telephone books, Mr. Bieringer encouraged others to meet the boats carrying refugees to Boston Harbor.

To meet his "resettlement" aim, Mr. Bieringer was instrumental in finding housing and jobs for refugees when they arrived in Boston. Within his extensive network of business colleagues, he would arrange a carefully selected match between one refugee and one businessman with the goal of having the businessman hire the refugee on a short-term basis. He worked tirelessly to persuade businesses to hire at least one refugee each, and he delivered this message in speeches and presentations around the country, stressing the richness and diverse contributions that the refugees would bring to a community. This last message addressed the third stage of the immigration process—adjustment to a new culture and environment.

Mr. Bieringer's involvement in refugee problems led him to the Window Shop, where he was a board member for a number of years. Although the "rescue" stage was most difficult for the Window Shop to engage in, a group of employees and board members did meet the boats and helped the refugees over the initial confusion and culture shock. The Window Shop's ability to offer jobs was critically important to this group—the Restaurant/Bakery and Gift Shop could offer extremely flexible work hours to accommodate the needs of the newcomers. The establishment of Friendship House,[73] which helped refugees ease the difficult transition to American life, was important to Mr. Bieringer, because it met the goal of "adjustment" to the new culture and environment.

In the aftermath of World War II, Mr. Bieringer's work with refugees increased. He was an adviser to President Truman on refugee affairs and a consultant to the State Department under President Eisenhower. He was chairman of the Governor's Commission on Refugees in Massachusetts in the late 1940s. He directed a relocation program for Japanese Americans who had been unjustly interned during the war, and he served as a U.S. delegate to the UN Conference on Refugees in the late 1960s. Mr. Bieringer was national head of the United Jewish Appeal and president of the United States Services for New Americans in 1950. Decades later, he was actively involved in the Boston-based educational organization, Facing History and Ourselves.

Mr. Bieringer's long-standing concern for African Americans took him to the Board of Trustees of Howard University in 1953. Closer to home, he chided his good friend and colleague on the Window Shop Board, Frank Vorenberg, president of Gilchrist's department store in Boston, for not hiring blacks. Later, Vorenberg invited him to the store and showed him a group of handsomely uniformed young black men hired as elevator operators. Bieringer was appalled. He suggested that the store hire several attractive, intelligent black women to work as sales associates on every floor. Thereafter, black employees were increasingly visible in downtown Boston stores.

On the board in 1964, Mr. Bieringer's business and refugee experience led him to question some of his colleagues' thinking and financial decisions, as well as the direction in which the Window Shop was headed. His gentle questions as to whether the capital could be used for more scholarships for the newcomers, whose need was great, came as a shock to other board members, who had been so involved in helping refugees in many ways and in expanding the organization. On January 28, 1970, Mr. Bieringer sent a letter of resignation to Board President Marion Bever. It came with "reluctance and a certain sense of sadness." He wrote:

> As you know, I have been a Director since the very inception of the Window Shop [through the Boston Committee for Refugees], and I enjoyed not only my participation in the fine accomplishments of the Window Shop in the past, but also my association with some very fine people.... For a long time, however, I have felt that the Window Shop had outlived its original purpose.... From the investment, it has been my judgment that there would be sufficient money to take care of some scholarships each year, without the headaches of fighting competition to stay alive.... Since so many members of the Board disagree with me, it is best that I step aside and wish you well.[74]

Within two years, the board found itself engulfed by management problems and serious competition from other businesses in Harvard Square. It reluctantly followed Mr. Bieringer's suggestion of selling the property and using its capital to enlarge the Scholarship Fund, thus helping to meet the growing needs of international students.

Alice DeNormandie Cope

Alice DeNormandie was born on July 25, 1909, and died April 29, 1994. Her father, Robert DeNormandie, was a Boston obstetrician. Her mother, Alice Brown DeNormandie, in addition to having been an excellent pianist when she was young, was very active in the Women's Suffrage movement and a founder and early president of the Massachusetts League of Women Voters.

Eliza Cope Harrison tells her mother's story in a letter to the authors in 2004:

> My mother went to the Winsor School in Boston; attended nursing school at Western Reserve University in Cleveland but did not feel particularly suited to nursing; then trained as a nursery school teacher at the Bank Street School in New York City.
>
> Immediately after she and my father, Oliver Cope, were married (in December 1932), they went to Germany. Their letters from that period describe what they saw in Berlin—including Nazi activities. These anti-Semitic acts were given immediacy when the professor with whom my father was working disappeared.
>
> They left Berlin and moved to London, where my father worked in Sir Henry Dale's laboratory. This was an immensely important, in fact life-changing, time in both my parents' lives. It was in London that they first began to help people who were leaving Germany. In London, they also became close friends of Charlotte and Harry Himsworth.

Ultimately, the Himsworths' two sons, John and Richard, came to live with our family in Cambridge during World War II.

Mother's firsthand understanding of what was happening in Europe obviously led directly to her concern for refugees, and of course to the Window Shop. The decision to add the two Himsworth children to our family, without any way of knowing when or what the end of the story would be, was bold, idealistic, and generous, and (I think) completely characteristic of her.

I remember mother loading all four of us, the Himsworths and [my brother] Bobby and me, into the old "beach wagon" (early version of a station wagon) to go to the Square and the Window Shop—the original one. People tended to be amazed that she toted us around with her, but somehow it was a great adventure and fun. I always felt comfortable with Mrs. Broch and the others, and then we always were offered cookies, combined with admonitions from Mother to say thank you and take only one.

Most remarkable to me, though, is that Mother made us understand why there was a Window Shop at all. She always provided the human background of what was going on, and why it was important. She linked what she and Daddy had seen at firsthand in Germany to what had happened to the (mostly) women at the Window Shop. She gave us details about who everyone was and what sort of lives they had led, and made it very clear to us—and I was only four or five in the beginning—what it meant to be uprooted, in the way they all were. As for the men, with "Hardy" [Professor Eberhard] Bruch and Mr. Benfey (I think it was he, but I'm not sure) as examples, she explained that distinguished teachers, lawyers, and judges like them would not be able to practice law in the United States—hence my first lesson in the difference between Roman and English law. More important, Mother told us what that could do to one's sense of one's self, to one's self-respect, and not least to one's ability to earn a living. In short, I think we all understood the profound respect and admiration she had for all the people who were creating and growing the Window Shop.

I also remember—but understood the details somewhat less—how much Mother enjoyed working with the others on the Window Shop Board, especially in the earliest years, when the challenges were so great and so exciting to them all…. I remember very vividly the discussions about whether they could afford to buy the Cock Horse/Brattle Street property. Mother was so thrilled when they worked it out—I'm sure everyone was—but Mother did have a story about how I had once said firmly that I wanted to be a "plain mother and no committees either!" But I think that was pre-Window Shop when I was about three years old. Since Mother told the story, I suppose she must have been worried about neglecting us, but I remember thinking to myself that it was sort of a silly thing for me to have said, if I said it.

Mother somehow made me, at least, a firm believer in the cause. As I've said, it was abundantly clear why the Window Shop was very important. It was equally obvious, of course, that it was all immensely exciting and for the most part great fun, for her particularly in the Shop's "formative" years. As far as I was concerned, it seemed natural that mothers did important things. What I didn't know until much more recently is that, unbeknownst to her, Mother was teaching the same lessons to several of my friends.

In her post-Window Shop years, Mother was especially active in the Family Service Association of Boston, and as a member of the national board of Family Service of America. She died on May 1, 1994.

Voices

"Board involvement with some of us was remarkable. Alice Cope, the president of the board, spent untold numbers of hours counseling and supporting. If not for her and Mary Mohrer, I would probably never have whipped up the courage to apply to the Columbia School of Social Work because of the expenses involved. Alice Cope assured me of the Window Shop's financial support if I needed it, while helping me file applications elsewhere. However, I was fortunate not to need its support, which, of course, made this money available to others.

"The Copes were so gracious in including some of us at parties at their home and had us stay at their beautiful summer family compound, Crowfield, in Rhode Island, when they felt we might benefit from an otherwise unaffordable vacation. These were indeed happy times."

Nadia Ehrlich Finkelstein

"I came to the U.S. in March 1947 from a displaced persons camp outside Munich. I joined my father in Dover, New Hampshire—he had gone into exile from Germany for political reasons in 1933. He had remarried, but was recently widowed, and had an eight- or nine-year-old son. I enrolled in the New Hampshire State College in Durham. I was nineteen and felt quite isolated in this new culture.

"One day Alice Cope came to see my father. She had helped him in the medical care of his wife, who had cancer. She and I took an instantaneous liking to each other. In her optimistic and hands-on way, she said, 'Charlotte, I'd like you to come to Cambridge for a visit.' I did go, and she took me to Filene's to buy some decent clothing. She said to me, 'You call me Alice,' and this was overwhelming to someone from Europe. On another visit, Alice said, 'Charlotte, I'd like to introduce you to Professor Ulich, who is a professor in the Education School at Harvard. Maybe you should go to school here.' I met with Ulich, and we hit it off. He suggested I apply to Radcliffe.

"I lived in the Copes' big attic room on Hubbard Park, worked at the Window Shop twenty-one hours a week and had my meals there. Alice and I were very close friends. After several months, going to Radcliffe and working at the Window Shop was more than I could handle. My father had returned to Germany—he was working on the new constitution—in the summer of 1949. Alice arranged for the boy [my brother], who was about eleven, to go to the Fenn School, and he too came to [live at] the Copes', where I took care of him. I barely got through my first year. I was struggling with these losses, my mother had died, I was trying to learn English, and at the end of my first year, I couldn't take my exams.

"I should say a word about the refugee situation. Most of the refugees I met and remember had family members in this country. They weren't alone. Alice must have been aware that I had nobody—my little brother went back to Germany after his year at Fenn. Alice's depth of understanding and her ability to tackle a problem and her commitment to it were extraordinary."

Charlotte Tejessy Sissman

"It is Alice to whom we were vitally connected over the years. [She insisted] that the Window Shop connect itself and its work to a larger sense of community.... The imperative to connect was overwhelming in the notes she dictated in the 1940s and 1950s when she, along with Sally Wolfinsohn, Frannie Fremont-Smith, and others interviewed newcomers in those early, tense days. Alice was tirelessly inventive in finding ways to approach immediate problems as basic as housing, food, money, education, and jobs.

"She was the pivotal person on a subcommittee in 1987 that labored to bring recommendations to the full board regarding the disbandment of the scholarship committee and the disbursement of its capital. Her continuing connectedness to the wide community helped us to identify the appropriate organizations that could continue what she and others had begun nearly fifty years earlier.

"That is a long span of time for one person to be so closely associated with one organization. Strictly speaking, she was not a 'founder' of the Window Shop. She surely was a priceless 'prime mover' very early, very often, and very well."

Dorothy Dahl

Dorothy Dahl

Dorothy Dahl was the only board member from the Pacific Northwest. She had come to Cambridge from Seattle for graduate work at Radcliffe, where she became interested in labor relations. She went to Princeton as a bride in 1943 and worked throughout the war as the first female research assistant in the Economic Department's Labor Relations Section. When her husband, Norman, returned from World War II and decided to pursue a Sc.D. at MIT, they returned to Cambridge. She accepted a job at the Peter Bent Brigham Hospital to establish and then run its first personnel department.

Because of this background, Board President Marion Bever suggested that Dorothy join the board to replace Bernice Cannon, who had long been responsible for personnel matters. She became a board member in 1954, and in 1962 the Dahls left for two years in Kanpur, India, where her husband set up a consortium in which nine American universities assisted in the development of the Indian Institute of Technology.

Upon their return in 1964, Dorothy Dahl became board president, involved with the transition between Alice Broch and Lotte Eisenberg, the new Restaurant manager from Israel, and the appointment of Mary Mohrer as general manager of the Window Shop. She left again for India in 1968, returning to Cambridge after the shop itself closed and the Window Shop Scholarship Fund began.

She was asked to be the president of that board in 1979 and enjoyed the connection with the college students and the new board members who interviewed them, as well as interactions with previous board members such as Mesdames Cope, Levin, Hermann, and Bever. During this presidency, she began the process of having board members interview past employees, board members, and customers for the Window Shop archives and worked with Katherine Kraft, the Schlesinger Library archivist, on the shop's papers.

During her long association with the Window Shop, Dorothy's energy and optimism were vital components of her leadership. As a board member and president, she was primarily concerned with the well-being of the employees and made certain that they were being treated fairly. Under Dorothy Dahl's leadership, the remaining scholarship funds were donated to other professional organizations whose personnel could continue the work that Window Shop volunteers had begun in 1944 with the Assistance Fund. For details of the distribution of funds, see Chapter 3.

Dorothy turned her energies to other community projects but, she says, "Nothing ever seemed to give me the pleasure that the Window Shop did." Her Window Shop interests continue today as a member of the personnel committee of the Cambridge Center for Adult Education. She occasionally finds herself giving informal Window Shop chats to people in the same space where the Gift and Dress Shop once was—about the Window Shop that once was.

Frances Fremont-Smith

In 1932, Frances Fremont-Smith was visiting in Germany. In an undated talk from the files of Dorothy Dahl, Mrs. Fremont-Smith said she saw "hooligans and swastikas everywhere." She had previously spent "a wonderful half-year with a family" in Heidelberg in 1926. By 1932, the young boys in the family were enrolled in the Hitler youth organization, and Mrs. Fremont-Smith returned to Cambridge very aware of the problems in Germany. She began looking for ways she could help, and at one time she worked on the assembly line of a local factory to aid the war effort.

Mrs. Fremont-Smith was an accomplished illustrator of children's books, and the author/illustrator of her own books, *Pablo's Pipe* and *The Traveling Coat*, published by E. P. Dutton in 1936 and 1937 respectively. At the age of eighteen, she married Dr. Frank Fremont-Smith, and they had three sons. The marriage ended in divorce in 1936.

She joined the board of directors of the Window Shop in 1941 and made a meaningful contribution by sponsoring Friendship House. In a 1984 interview, Alice Cope said of her good friend:

> Franny was always on the board. She was secretary for years. Everybody loved her. She was not only intelligent and kind, she was also a born teacher. She helped a lot of the women learning English....
>
> Franny was wonderful with the women because she's one of these people who genuinely loves all other people. She never went to college. Her grandfather was President Eliot of Harvard University. She was married when she was barely eighteen. In a way she never had a chance to be herself because she was married so young and then she had these little boys one right after the other.

Mrs. Fremont-Smith died in Lexington, Massachusetts, in 1998 at the age of 96.

Bessie Zaban Jones

"Ounce for ounce, pound for pound, Bessie had more than anybody else—more energy, more interests, more passion, more brains," said former Board President Dorothy Dahl at a celebration of Mrs. Jones's life on May 31, 1997. Professor Howard Mumford Jones of Harvard University described his wife as "short, merry-faced with a sense of mischief. She expected more of life than mere entertainment."

Bessie Jones's early acquaintance with the Window Shop is described in Chapter 1. She once referred to her deep concern for refugees as "an affair of the blood."

With this concern added to her background in academia, advertising, and retail, she made many new connections between the Window Shop and others. She interested her friend Margaret Earhart Smith in the new shop; she asked her niece Adele Brager, a retail buyer and store owner, to lend her experience to the talented but inexperienced Mary Mohrer in the Gift and Dress Shop; and at a Cambridge dinner party, she told the dean of the Harvard Business School that the struggling Tea Room was having trouble getting sugar under wartime rationing. He replied that he was on the board of a local dextrose plant, and he saw to it that a hundred pounds were delivered the next day. The shipments continued at intervals throughout the war. In addition, the Joneses discovered the department store Den Permanente in Copenhagen on their travels, made friends with the owners, and paved the way for Mary Mohrer to purchase unique items there to be sold at the Window Shop.

Mrs. Jones's time on the board was not without drama. She abhorred committees and their meetings. Her colleagues on the executive committee in the early 1940s were mostly without work experience and, as amateurs, viewed the emerging Shop, Restaurant and Bakery, as a needed social agency. Records show her leaving the board because of their lack of professionalism, but she almost always returned quickly to help when it was needed.

Her interest in and concern for the plight of refugees continued throughout her life and in her writing. She wrote a biography of famed astronomer Dr. Harlow Shapley, who secured academic appointments at Harvard University for refugees.[75] Among her other published works are *Louisa May Alcott: Hospital Sketches*,[76] and *Lighthouse of the Skies: The Smithsonian Astrophysical Observatory: Background and History, 1846–1955*.[77] With her husband, Mrs. Jones edited *The Many Voices of Boston: A Historical Anthology*.[78]

Bessie Jones stayed active until the age of ninety-nine, still petite, still intense, and in the words of Dorothy Dahl, "still, I hope, aware of the deep contributions she had made to others."

Margaret Earhart Smith

Mrs. Smith was named the first president of the Window Shop board of directors in February 1940 and was one of the incorporators in 1941. She quickly appointed a sub-committee (of which she was a member) to handle the daily business of the Window Shop. Under her leadership, the first manager of the Restaurant/Bakery was hired, and the board negotiated a lease at 102 Mount Auburn—a key move. It was under Mrs. Smith's guidance and thanks to her vision that the foundation was laid for the Window Shop's future success.

She had been a very early supporter of the enterprise, recruited by her friend Bessie Jones. Mrs. Smith clearly understood the double set of cultures that inhabited the early Window Shop—the obvious one of European refugees and the established American community. In a letter to Elsa Ulich, she wrote: "Two different cultures are trying to operate through the Window Shop that have not yet learned how to run well in double harness.... The Window Shop has interested me because in functioning as a shop, it has performed social services, but it seems to me that its continuance depends upon its being primarily a good shop."[79] This conversation lasted until the Window Shop closed, and probably no single person had such an innate understanding of each part of the whole.

Mrs. Smith was born in 1902, graduated from Vassar College, and in 1949 was elected to the Radcliffe Board of Trustees. She was married to Dr. Clement A. Smith, associate professor of pediatrics at Harvard Medical School. In 1942, the Smiths moved to Detroit, where Dr. Smith took a new job, and Mrs. Smith enrolled in the University of Michigan School of Social Work, where she earned her master's degree. She became especially interested in labor relations and race relations. When the Smiths returned to Cambridge in 1945, Mrs. Smith became involved in many social agencies, boards, and committees, and also taught adult education courses. She was a valued teacher in these years, especially on the relationships between the community and its organizations.

Even after she resigned as president, Mrs. Smith was able to put her own imprimatur on the Window Shop. She identified areas in which the Gift and Dress Shop and the Restaurant could be improved and suggested standardization of quality in both. She resigned from the board in 1946.

Alice Cope, who became president in 1948, said of her predecessor, "She was a teacher, and a great one. Her eager, curious, and wide-ranging mind made her ask questions everywhere. In asking questions and seeking answers, she taught whomever she touched."

At the death of Mrs. Smith in 1964, Mrs. Cope said:

> Margaret Smith gave the Window Shop a firm foundation which makes it, twenty-five years later, an important example of intercultural and interracial cooperation. She insisted that the Window Shop should not be just a gift shop and restaurant operated for profit, but a place where people of varied races, religions, and backgrounds might work together, providing living proof that we are one world. She was largely responsible for the vision and practical plan which made this possible.

Another board member said, "She had no use for 'administration by committee' and vigorously said so. One of her great gifts was the ability to delegate a job and leave it to be done. She taught many others how important is this simple administrative principle."

Said another, "Margaret Smith possessed virtues enough for three women; she had a keen mind and an unerring sense of the right course. She was buoyant, vigorous, and cheerful, and she cared deeply for people, to whom she gave unsparingly of her understanding, sympathy, and kindness."

The *Radcliffe Quarterly*, the college's alumnae magazine, wrote: "On the more personal side, she wears chic hats, drives a Jaguar, reads, and travels widely."[80] Mrs. Smith's energy and vision resulted in the expansion of Radcliffe's Management Training Program, which she helped transform into the Harvard-Radcliffe Program in Business Administration.

There is no doubt that Margaret Earhart Smith was one of the most important figures in the history of the Window Shop. She set higher standards for both the Gift and Dress Shop and the Restaurant and steered the enterprise on a solid path before turning over its operation and management to others.

To the ever-eloquent Alice Cope belongs the last word:

> To everything upon which her eye or heart or mind rested she brought clear thinking, lively humor, a wonderful turn of phrase, and wise comment. She had both the ability to be indignant and the ability to be patient. She had charm and grace, wit and humor, sensitiveness and shyness, all of which made her loved and admired whether one agreed with her or not.

Elsa Brändström Ulich

Among all the visionary figures who guided and influenced the Window Shop, Elsa Brändström stands out as a larger-than-life inspiration. "She gave courage and stimulation to this board and to the workers," said Alice Cope, who succeeded her as president. Before she even arrived in Cambridge in 1933, she was known internationally for her work with prisoners of war in Siberia.

The force of her personality and will cannot be overstated. "She radiates light," commented one admirer. Elsa Brändström, born in 1888, was the daughter of the Swedish military attaché in St. Petersburg, Russia. The family returned to Ostergotland, Sweden, in 1891, where Elsa was educated. In 1906 her father was appointed Swedish ambassador to the Court of the Tsar in St. Petersburg. Elsa stayed in Stockholm to study, hoping to fulfill her dream of opening her own adult education center. This dream was set aside when the principal told her that she could never hope to be a teacher because the subjects taught did not interest her. "She was excited about the present, about social and political problems for live people," writes her biographer. Elsa began to travel with her father, to learn many languages, and to throw herself into the social and cultural life of St. Petersburg of the early 1900s.

On July 31, 1914, Germany declared war on Russia. In August, large transports of wounded Russian soldiers began arriving in St. Petersburg, now called Petrograd. Elsa trained to become a nurse and dedicated herself to caring for the wounded soldiers. Her care later extended to German prisoners of war, especially those who were transported to Siberia. She felt an affinity with the Germans and saw them in distress, wounded, in enemy territory. She and a fellow nurse collected clothing, food, and medicine for the prisoners before they were transported east to Siberia.

By October 1915, Elsa wore the uniform of the Swedish Red Cross and with her nursing friend traveled to Siberia to minister to the prisoners. For nearly three years the two women fought illness, cold, and deplorable conditions to give humanitarian aid to the prisoners. Elsa became known as "The Angel of Siberia." She did not leave Siberia until the German prisoners of war were returned to their homeland after the war. Elsa had promised those who were near death that she would look after their dependents in Germany. To raise funds, she went on a lecture tour of the United States, and with the proceeds she founded two homes in Germany: a convalescent home in Marienborn for returning invalids without a family, and a children's home, Neusorge, for orphans of prisoners of war. During this time, she met Professor Robert Ulich, an official in the German Ministry of Education in Dresden. In November 1929 they were married in Marienborn and in January 1932, their daughter, Brita, was born.

When Hitler came to power in 1933, the Ulichs left Germany. Professor Ulich lectured in England and was soon offered a professorship at Harvard University. He and his wife settled in Cambridge in 1933, at a time when refugees from Hitler's Europe were beginning to arrive. Elsa's work was clear to her—new refugees needed help. She procured hundreds of affidavits for refugees to enter the United States, over time welcomed more than a hundred in her home, and found boarding houses where they could recuperate. Cambridge friends made their homes available to her, and other "guest houses" were found in the Boston area where most of the refugee ships landed. Elsa checked in with the refugees almost every day, knew them all, and was interested in every detail of their lives. In addition to finding shelter for the refugees, she devoted considerable energies to finding jobs for them—and along the way, gave comfort and hope to many.

Through her refugee work, Elsa Ulich found the Window Shop and immersed herself in its mission. She became a member of the first board of directors after incorporation in 1941. In 1942, the board asked Elsa Ulich to become its president.

Significant innovations under Elsa Ulich's term included the establishment of the Assistance Fund and Friendship House and the expansion of counseling services. Under her leadership and energy, the Window Shop helped refugees with numerous services including education, retraining, housing, furnishings, personal problems, illnesses, recreation, and citizenship training.

Elsa Brändström Ulich died on March 4, 1948. She left a vibrant, self-supporting, nonprofit institution that served as her memorial.[81]

Voices

"Again and again it happened to me at parties in Boston and Cambridge that the hostess whispered in my ear: 'It is amazing—the minute your wife enters the room it is as if someone lighted a candle; she radiates light.' And indeed, that was her deepest mysterious gift, a charisma one would falsify if one wanted to analyze it."

Professor Robert Ulich

"Elsa and Robert invited everyone who came to them into their home—some stayed for a cup of tea, others stayed for weeks. All went away with renewed hope and understanding, for Elsa interpreted America to them. She softened the blows of reality; she gave sound, practical help and advice. She found jobs and homes and friends for hundreds.... This work was her triumph. It had no excitement, no romance, no prestige. It was unpopular; it was thwarted at every turn by prejudice and inhospitality. These refugees were the unwanted, the misunderstood, the needy.

"She learned American customs and with vivid imagination and quick wit translated them to the refugees who found America bewildering. She told them accurately and boldly what they would and would not find and still found the way to soften for them the inevitable blows of reality. If we now look with pride at those many new citizens who came to us because of Hitler, we must gratefully acknowledge that many of them have found their way because of some work or action of Elsa Brändström Ulich."

Alice Cope

"It had to happen that my wife was quickly drawn into all kinds of welfare work for the steadily growing numbers of mostly Jewish refugees. If they were lucky, they arrived in the United States with ten dollars. From breakfast to supper, visitors appeared at our house. The second floor in Walker Street was always inhabited by refugees. I still remember our little daughter Brita, asking once, 'Mutti, couldn't we once sit together at lunch for a few minutes without the telephone ringing?'"

Professor Robert Ulich

"It never occurred to her that something could not be done. She used to say, 'If you can't get in one door, go around to another.' Like all strong-minded, full-of-ideas people, she was sometimes overpowering. All one needed to say was, 'Now, Elsa, wait a minute,' and she would.

"When she discovered the slowly growing Window Shop, she was delighted. It was just the kind of slightly crazy, impossible job she loved to be a part of. She was enormously impressed with the Gift Shop/Dress Shop, which was growing, buying from various new Americans with special skills, and becoming well known in Cambridge.

"She was proud that we are a group of Jews and non-Jews working together."

Alice Cope

"She demanded much from others but never anything she was not willing to show how to do and then to perform it. When the Window Shop, a cooperative enterprise and kind of self-help operation, threatened to get stuck in all the difficulties of the beginnings, Elsa Brändström helped out, serving the guests in the Restaurant."

Professor Robert Ulich

"Mrs. Ulich believed that people could learn to work together despite varying temperaments, backgrounds, and personalities. As if by miracle, the waitresses and the kitchen staff forgot their differences and did work together. If shortage of help in the kitchen meant the pots and pans must be washed, Mrs. Ulich rolled up her sleeves and washed them. At first the staff was shocked. Ladies didn't do so in Europe. Then they thought, if Mrs. Ulich could do such things it was right for them to pitch in and do what was necessary, whether [it was] their job or not. She invited the workers to her home and learned their stories. Each week she had an office hour when anyone could talk to her alone. They all adored her. She was a heroine. She, too, was a refugee. She spoke German. She really knew them. She understood how very hard it was to make your way in a strange land."

Marion Muller

"Somehow during the move [to Brattle Street] the attic had not been cleaned out, and its cleaning was such a chore that no one had gotten around to it. So Mrs. Ulich and Mrs. Cope armed themselves with brooms, rags, and mops, rolled up their sleeves, and cleaned it. This action on the part of two *Frau Professors* was extraordinary to people newly come from the stratified world of Germany and Austria. The tradition of volunteer board members getting their hands dirty continued all the years that we ran a Bakery, a Restaurant, and a Gift and Dress Shop."

Dorothy Dahl

Sally Wolfinsohn

According to her daughter, Judy Wolfinsohn Parker, Sally Wolfinsohn "seemed to live and breathe the Shop, especially during the '40s and '50s when it was growing, and the need was greatest. She and my father had moved from New York to Cambridge in the fall of 1939 (for three years, they thought, but they never left), and my mother was looking for activities to get involved in. I don't remember how she found out about the Shop, but recall her talking about some wonderful women she'd met who were knitting things and making clothes in an upstairs room on Church Street.

"The *raison d'être* of the Shop was right up my mother's street. Her American parents—particularly her father, Cyrus Adler—had been well-known Jewish educators and activists. She considered herself lucky to be American, and as such she felt bound to do something to help refugees from Hitler—Jewish or not. Here was a chance to exercise her administrative and managerial skills—besides her compassion for people who had been uprooted by the war. She was very involved in the Shop's move to Mount Auburn Street and its subsequent move to the Blacksmith House."

When Alice Cope became president in 1948, she worked closely with Mrs. Wolfinsohn. "My mother was vice president, then and forever," said Ms. Parker. "She always refused the presidency; she said she couldn't deal with the responsibility. She could have easily, of course, but she was modest and feared confrontation and hated giving orders—which came naturally to Alice, who was a forceful person. Besides other duties, managing the Scholarship Fund was the perfect job for Mom … deciding who was most worthy, how much they should get, and for how long."

Sally Wolfinsohn became close friends with several women she helped. One was Ilona Karmel, a Polish writer who went through Radcliffe partly with Window Shop aid. She was a concentration camp survivor and was enormously talented. "My mother became Ilona's American mother," recalls Ms. Parker. "Until Ilona got married, she lived with us on and off. My mother edited her first novel, *Stephania*, which she had begun at Radcliffe while studying with Archibald MacLeish."

The shop was a community that constantly brought people together, Ms. Parker recalled. "We ate its food, wore its clothes, bought its first unique merchandise, served its fabulous desserts at our parties. The board members and their spouses knew each other well and often socialized. But like any workplace, the Shop had personnel problems. My mother would agonize over them. She'd come home and tell us who had said what to whom, and what could be done about it.

She hated any kind of unpleasantness, even though she herself could be very tart. Still, she often found herself having to negotiate a truce.

"In spite of additional responsibilities, my mother remained committed to the Shop in the '60s and early '70s. She doled out funds to Hungarian and Asian immigrants and worked closely with Elizabeth Aub and Dorothy Dahl. I moved away from Cambridge in 1960, but returned in 1968. I remember my mother being concerned and angry with the Shop's new financial managers. I didn't know much about them so I was stunned when she told me the Shop was going to close. 'We were doing okay until those young Harvard Business School grads took over and ruined everything,' she said. 'They didn't understand us.'"

Charlotte Tejessy Sissman, who lived with the Wolfinsohns and with the Copes while she studied at Radcliffe said, "Sally was one of the most beautiful women I ever met. She was reserved, but she had a strong social presence and a mind of her own. She was generous and very hospitable."

Gisela Wyzanski

Mrs. Wyzanski was an international figure who helped thousands of Jewish children leave Nazi Germany before World War II. From 1935 to 1938, she worked out of the Berlin office of Youth Aliyah, arranging for visas, transportation, and new homes for Jewish children in Palestine, Britain, and Sweden. In 1938 she opened a temporary center in England for refugee children and returned to Berlin. The following year she came to the United States.

During the war years, Mrs. Wyzanski served as vice chairman and chairman of Youth Aliyah and as a national board member of Hadassah. She devoted herself to UNICEF, becoming virtually a full-time volunteer, and her obituary in the *Boston Globe* of June 6, 1991, lists almost a dozen other organizations in which she held a leading role.

She still found time to devote to the Window Shop, becoming a board member in 1944. According to former Board President Dorothy Dahl, "Gisela was a dynamo in the smallest permissible package.... She was unbending in making central to all decisions a Window Shop employee's individual and family situation."

Mrs. Wyzanski was the author of persuasive letters for the Window Shop's annual appeal, which drew compliments from board members and generous donations from their recipients. She was married to the Honorable Charles E. Wyzanski Jr. of the United States District Court in Boston. He died in 1986.

After his mother's death, Charles M. Wyzanski wrote: "So many people from so many walks of life were touched by Mother's goodness that surely, if there is a heaven, she will be offered prompt admission. I'm only afraid she won't be happy there—not enough souls in need of her marvelous capacity to do and to help."

Appendix
Window Shop Archive at the
Schlesinger Library

MC 427 THE WINDOW SHOP, INC., 1939–87

The Window Shop records at the Schlesinger Library were donated by various officers and processed by archivist Katherine Gray Kraft in 1994. They cover the years 1939–92, measure about fifteen shelf feet, and are arranged in three series: I. Organization and history; II. Administration; and III. Program. Some documents are temporarily closed to research to protect the privacy of employees and aid recipients; in a few cases, copies of such documents with the sensitive information removed are available.

Series I contains the articles of incorporation; by-laws; papers regarding the tenth and twentieth anniversaries; and histories and articles about the Window Shop or on related topics. Oral histories, most conducted by board members in 1984–85, provide information about board members and staff; employees discuss immigrating, how they found the Window Shop, their work there, friendships, relations with customers, etc. The histories and articles in this series provide conflicting information about dates and events; the financial statements and board minutes in Series II are more reliable sources.

Series II includes minutes of the executive committee and board of directors, lists of board members and a few photographs, some committee reports, correspondence (board, general, and about the dissolution), board mailings (memos, reports, agendas, etc.), presidents' annual reports, Elizabeth Aub's appointment book/diary entries, financial records, filings for government agencies, and public relations materials. Both the minutes of the executive committee and the Elizabeth Aub appointment book/diary entries contain information about employees and applicants for assistance and their problems, and so are closed to research for seventy-five years. The board minutes and correspondence are good sources for following the evolution of purpose and approach to the refugee situation, including philosophical disagreements about treatment of employees, financial and other difficulties of expansion, and problems encountered by the restaurant business. The board's subject correspondence documents the cooperation between the Window Shop and other refugee-aid and Cambridge organizations, work for displaced persons legislation, and Eleanor Roosevelt's visit in 1950.

The extensive financial records provide another window on the Window Shop's changing fortunes and include the 1939 financial statements, which, along with an account book, are the earliest records of the Window Shop. Public relations materials include not only advertisements and leaflets, but also place mats, menu, stationery, the rocking horse insignia designed by Gyorgy Kepes, and a (dismantled) publicity scrapbook.

Series III documents other early refugee projects and Window Shop Gift Shop and Restaurant operations. It includes extensive personnel and pension records; legal documents, correspondence, and architectural plans for buildings and alterations; and records of the assistance funds. Aside from restricted personnel files, there are documents on personnel practices: advice to employees, wage rates, minutes, and reports of the personnel practices committee, etc. A major portion of this series concerns the collection and dispersal of the assistance funds; it consists of reports, fund appeals, records of contributors and the scholarship committee (including restricted case files and other references to aid recipients), and statistics on scholarship recipients.

Eva Moseley, archivist, the Schlesinger Library

Voices of the Window Shop

Listed below are individuals who are quoted in this book, in addition to other key personnel at the Window Shop.

<u>Name</u>	<u>Position</u>	<u>Years</u>
Robert Alexander & Jack Alexander	Sons of Fred Alexander Grandsons of Hertha Becher	
Elizabeth Aub	President Board member	1954–64 1942–77
Henry Beauvais	Chef, Restaurant	1971
Hertha Becher	Cashier, Restaurant	1943–68
Walter Bieringer	Board member	1941–70
Lucille Bell	Sales assistant, Gift Shop	1955
Lotte Benfey	Assistant manager, Restaurant	1945–64
Robert Berger, M.D.	Scholarship recipient	1950
Marion Bever	Board member President	1939–87 1968–72
Alice Boehm	Dressmaker, Gift Shop	1940–50
Alice Broch	Manager, Restaurant	1939–64
Julian Bussgang	Scholarship recipient	1949
Alice DeNormandie Cope	President Board member	1948–54 1940–69
Dorothy Dahl	President President Board member	1964–68 1979–87 1955–87

Name	Position	Years
Lotte Eisenberg	Manager, Restaurant	1964–65
Nadia Ehrlich Finkelstein	Waitress, Restaurant	1948–50s
Frances Fremont-Smith	Board member	1941–72
Anne Glace	Kitchen supervisor	Late 1960s
Guy Greco	Manager, Restaurant	1970–71
Mary Halevy	Sales assistant, Gift Shop	1960s
Anne Harken	Board member President	1974–87 1974–79
Deborah Hermann	Board member	1950–87
Ilse Heyman	Assistant manager, Gift Shop	1947–72
Bessie Jones	Board member Manager, Gift Shop	1944–50 1939–42
Richard Kahan	President	1972–74
Lillian Cohan Levin	Board member	1940s–72
Elisabeth Martens	Assistant manager, Restaurant	1942–67
Doris Martin	Waitress, head baker, Restaurant	1952–87
Mary Mohrer	Manager, Gift Shop	1939–72
Pearl Morrison	Waitress, Bakery assistant, Restaurant	1963–87
Marion Muller	Board member	1940s, 1950s
Judith Wolfinsohn Parker	Sales assistant, Gift Shop	1950s
Olga Schiffer	Baker, Restaurant	1939–42

Name	Position	Years
Denise Serres	Sales assistant, Gift Shop	1970–72
Charlotte Tejessy Sissman	Waitress, Restaurant	1949–50s
Margaret Earhart Smith	President Board member	1941–42 1941–46
Hedy Sturges	Board member	1950–72
Marie Swanson	Sales assistant, Gift Shop	1950s
Elsa Brändström Ulich	President	1942–48
Jack Vissel	Manager, Restaurant	1968–69
Martha Washington	Cook, Restaurant	1950s–60s
Sally Wolfinsohn	Board member	1940s–74
Henry Wurmfeld	Chef, Restaurant	1953–71
Tamar Wurmfeld	Waitress, Restaurant Sales assistant, Gift Shop	1954–72
Ilona Karmel Zucker	Scholarship recipient	1948

Recipes from the Window Shop Bakery

Longtime Head Baker Doris Martin has shared the following recipes with us.

Linzer Torte (Mrs. Broch's family recipe)

7 ounces butter	Peel of one lemon, grated
5 1/2 ounces sugar	3/4 teaspoon vanilla extract
1/4 cup egg yolks (about 3–4),	6 ounces ground walnuts
separated (save egg whites)	9 ounces all-purpose flour
1/2 teaspoon each cinnamon, nutmeg,	8 ounces raspberry or apricot
and ground cloves	preserves

Preheat oven to 350°. Beat in large bowl butter, sugar, and egg yolks until creamy. Add the three spices, lemon peel, and vanilla extract. Add walnuts; mix well. Mix in flour. Refrigerate dough for 1/2 hour. Roll out approximately 2/3 of dough. Cover bottom and sides of 8-inch pan with dough. Fill with preserves. Roll out remaining 1/3 dough into 1/4-inch-wide strips and place in lattice pattern over jam. Brush strips with egg whites as glaze. Bake at 350° for approximately one hour until golden brown.

Plum Tart

12 ounces (approximately) *Murbteig* (see below)
26 Italian plums (available *only* in September)
Streusel (optional, see below)

Murbteig:

11 ounces all-purpose flour
3 1/2 ounces sugar
Peel of one lemon, grated

8 ounces margarine or butter
1/4 cup egg yolks (about 3–4)
1/2 teaspoon vanilla extract

For Murbteig:
Mix butter or margarine with sugar and yolks until creamy. Add flour, lemon peel and vanilla extract. Mix until dough stays together. Refrigerate for 1/2 hour.

Streusel:

2 tablespoons flour
2 tablespoons butter

4 tablespoons sugar
1/2 teaspoon cinnamon

For Streusel:
Mix ingredients using fingertips until small crumbs are formed.

Preheat oven to 350°. Line 8-inch pie plate with *Murbteig*. Slice plums into quarters and remove pits. Fill pie plate with quartered plums, standing up. Sprinkle with Streusel. Bake at 350° until plums are soft, about 40 minutes. If needed for sweetness, sprinkle with 1 tablespoon sugar.

Vanilla Cookies

(Makes about 5 dozen cookies)
9 ounces each butter and margarine
7 ounces granulated sugar
3 ounces ground walnuts
3 1/2 ounces ground hazelnuts (filberts)
1 pound 10 ounces all-purpose flour
Vanilla sugar

Preheat oven to 325°. Mix butter, margarine, and granulated sugar until creamy. Add walnuts and hazelnuts. Add flour and mix well. Refrigerate dough for about 20 minutes. Roll out dough to 1/2-inch thickness. Use crescent cookie cutter or any other cutter. Place cookies on greased cookie sheet. Bake in 325° oven for about 20 minutes until edges are lightly browned. After baking, sprinkle with vanilla sugar.

Blitz Torte

1 1/2 ounces butter
3 ounces sugar
3 egg yolks (reserve whites for meringue)
1/4 cup light cream

4 ounces pastry or cake flour
1 1/2 teaspoon baking powder
1 cup sliced almonds

Preheat oven to 300°. Cream together butter and sugar. Add egg yolks; beat until light and fluffy. Add cream, flour, and baking powder and mix until flour is dissolved. Pour batter into two 8-inch greased pie pans.

For meringue:
3 egg whites
3/4 cup sugar

Pinch of cream of tartar
1 teaspoon almond extract

Beat egg whites until stiff. Add sugar slowly. Add cream of tartar and almond extract. Spread meringue on top of each of the two pans of batter, then sprinkle about 2/3 of the sliced almonds on top of one pan. Bake at 300° for 30 minutes. Turn out on racks and let cool. Place layer without almonds on a plate, spread cream filling (below) on top of it. Reserve a bit for spreading outside of cake and then place layer with almonds on top.

For cream filling:
1 whole egg
2 1/2 tablespoons sugar
1 cup sour cream
1 scant tablespoon cornstarch
1 lemon rind, grated

Whisk egg, sugar, sour cream, and cornstarch in double boiler until thick. Cool and then add lemon rind.

For outside of cake, spread cream filling on sides and place remaining almond slices around it.

Emperor Cake

7 egg yolks
6 ounces sugar
5 egg whites
6 ounces hazelnuts, ground

4 ounces bittersweet chocolate, diced
(Callebaut is recommended)
2 ounces flour
Glacé cherries
Sliced almonds

Preheat oven to 350°. Grease two 8-inch round pans. Beat yolks and sugar until light and fluffy. Beat egg whites until stiff. Fold half of whites into yolk mixture. Mix nuts, chocolate, and flour and fold into egg mixture. Fold in remaining egg whites.

Divide and place into prepared cake pans. Bake at 350° for 25 minutes until cake loosens from pans. Place on rack to cool.

Make buttercream filling (below). Spread filling between two layers. (An option is to cut each layer in half horizontally, ending up with four layers. Divide filling between three layers and spread evenly.) Apricot jam may be substituted for buttercream filling. Spread chocolate frosting (below) on top layer.

For buttercream filling:
1/2 cup butter
4 cups confectioners' sugar, sifted
4 ounces unsweetened chocolate,
melted (Calebaut is recommended)

1 egg
1/8 teaspoon salt
1 teaspoon vanilla extract
4 tablespoons light cream

Cream butter until light and fluffy. Gradually add half of sugar, adding melted unsweetened chocolate with each addition of sugar. Beat well after each addition. Blend in egg, salt, and vanilla. Add remaining sugar, alternating with cream. Beat until smooth after each addition.

For chocolate frosting:
1/2 cup light corn syrup
6 tablespoons water

5 tablespoons butter
12 ounces semisweet chocolate bits

Combine corn syrup, water, and butter in a heavy saucepan. Bring to a rapid boil, stirring until butter is melted. Remove from heat. Add chocolate, stirring until completely melted. Cool to room temperature. Then spread over cake. Decorate top with glacé cherries and sliced almonds.

Chocolate Cherry Cake

1/4 pound butter
1 cup sugar
2 eggs
2 tablespoons cocoa
1/2 cup ground walnuts

1 teaspoon vanilla extract
1/2 cup flour
1 teaspoon baking powder
1 can sour cherries, drained well

Preheat oven to 350°. Grease a 9-inch springform pan. Cream butter and sugar. Add eggs, cocoa, nuts, and vanilla. Mix flour and baking powder and add to batter. Pour into prepared springform pan. Put well-drained cherries on top of batter, evenly distributed. Bake about 40 to 45 minutes. Can be covered with chocolate frosting. Serve with whipped cream.

Notes

1   The best-known consignment shop for refugees outside of Cambridge was in New York City. Called Trade Winds, it operated from 1939 to 1941.

2   Schlesinger, Marion Cannon, *Snatched from Oblivion* (Boston: Little, Brown & Company, 1949), 79.

3   Ibid, 79–80.

4   Telephone interview of Arnold Schutzberg of East Cambridge, Mass., by Ellen Miller, December 4, 2003.

5   Historian and Professor Stephen H. Norwood of the University of Oklahoma made headlines in November 2004 when he presented a paper at a Boston University conference detailing Harvard's record of "helping to legitimize the evil Nazi regime." Norwood charged that Harvard, unlike other major universities, offered no positions to Jewish refugee scholars who came to the United States in the 1930s under the auspices of the Emergency Committee in Aid of Displaced German Scholars. Dr. Rafael Medoff and Benyamin Korn, "How Harvard Could Have Responded to the Nazis," The David Wyman Institute for Holocaust Studies, December 2004. In their book, *Making Harvard Modern* (Oxford: Oxford University Press, 2001), coauthors Morton Keller and Phyllis Keller also describe Harvard's stance on refugee scholars.

6   Keller, Morton and Phyllis, *Making Harvard Modern* (Oxford: Oxford University Press, 2001).

7   Dershowitz, Alan, *Chutzpah* (Boston: Little, Brown & Co., 1991), 65.

8   Johnson, Paul, *History of the Jews* (New York: Random House, 1990), 503.

9   *Harvard Crimson*, February 24, 1939.

10   *Harvard Crimson*, February 6, 1939.

11   Jones, Bessie Zaban "To the Rescue of the Learned: The Asylum Fellowship Plan at Harvard, 1938–40," *Harvard Library Bulletin*, Summer 1984, 205–38.

12   *Harvard Crimson*, November 22, 1938.

13 Lahiri was awarded the Pulitzer Prize in 2000 for her book of short stories about the immigrant experience, *Interpreter of Maladies* (Boston: Houghton Mifflin, 2000). She is also the author of *The Namesake* (Boston: Houghton Mifflin, 2003).

14 James McLaughlin was a professor at Harvard Law School, and Professor Willard van Orman Quine was a professor of Symbolic Logic at Harvard College who, in the 1940s, became one of America's leading philosophers. Mrs. Griffin's husband was reported to be a member of the Classics faculty at Harvard, but this information cannot be verified, nor has any identification of Mrs. Carpenter's husband and his connection with Harvard University been confirmed.

15 Account book in the Window Shop Archives, Schlesinger Library, box 1, folder 25.

16 "The Story of the Window Shop, Presented to the Cambridge Historical Society" by Mrs. Oliver Cope, November 17, 1974.

17 The incorporators of the Window Shop were Margaret S. Blumgart, Alice Cope, Charles F. Dunbar, William Ehrlich, Helen M. Eisemann, Margaret Earhart Smith, F. Frank Vorenberg, and Bessie Z. Jones.

18 Among the very active Boston-area organizations for refugees in the late 1930s were the Cambridge Refugee Guest House on Franklin Street, the Boston Committee for Refugees, the Council of Jewish Women, Jewish Philanthropies, and the New England Christian Committee.

19 Replacing the original founders of the Window Shop prior to incorporation in 1941 were Bessie Jones, Johnnie Fainsod, Frances Fremont-Smith, Alice Cope, Marion Bever, Elsa Brändström Ulich, and Sally Wolfinsohn. The husbands of these women were either local professors or prominent Cambridge residents.

20 Letter from Alice Perutz and Olga Schiffer to executive committee, February 22, 1941.

21 Letter from Margaret Smith to Elsa Ulich, January 15, 1941.

22 Professor Richard von Mises was the Gordon-McKay Professor of Aerodynamics and Applied Mathematics at Harvard. Professor Werner Jaeger was director of the Institute for Classical Studies at Harvard. Both men left Nazi Germany in the early 1930s and were well-known in their respective fields.

23 Kepes was an internationally recognized painter, sculptor, and photographer. In 1967 he founded the Center for Advanced Visual Studies at MIT, a

community that would unite the work of artists and designers with that of architects, engineers, city planners, and scientists; he served as director until 1972. His writings include *Language of Vision* (1944) and *The New Landscape in Art and Science* (1956).

24   Compiled by Ruth V. Noble and published by the Berkshire Publishing Company of Cambridge, Mass. Jean E. Nathan kindly called this book to our attention.

25   Alice Cope, speech to the Winsor School, May 9, 1951.

26   Ibid.

27   Interview of Mary Mohrer, October 16, 1984.

28   Alice Cope, speech to the Winsor School, May 9, 1951.

29   Marion Muller, paper read at the Mothers' Study Club, Cambridge, April 1959.

30   Marion Muller, Twentieth Anniversary Talk, April 1959.

31   President's Report by Elizabeth Aub, May 1964.

32   Among the relief organizations were the American-Hungarian Federation, Catholic Relief Services, Church World Services, Hungarian League of America, and the International Rescue Committee.

33   Twenty-eight years later, when the (Ulich) Scholarship Fund disbanded in 1987, awards for the years 1972 to 1987 showed another seismic shift. Students came from seventy-nine countries, the largest number being from Africa (43 percent), and the smallest from Europe (7.5 percent). In between were the Near East (half from Iran) (16.5 percent), Russia (15 percent), Asia (10.5 percent), the Americas (7.5 percent).

34   Note by Board President Elizabeth Aub, January 1964.

35   Board of directors meeting, October 26, 1964.

36   Letter from Walter Bieringer to Alice Cope, October 28, 1964.

37   Report to executive committee by Mary Mohrer, March 23, 1965.

38   Ibid.

39   Executive committee report, April 12, 1966.

40   Executive committee report, June 7, 1966.

41   Executive committee report, March 1, 1966.

42   Executive committee report, April 26, 1966.

43   Executive committee report, January 3, 1967.

44　Board of directors meeting, November 16, 1966.

45　Executive committee report, October 17, 1967.

46　Annual meeting, board of directors, April 6, 1970.

47　Executive committee report, October 29, 1968.

48　Executive committee report, December 3, 1968.

49　Annual meeting, board of directors, April 6, 1970.

50　Executive committee report, January 20, 1970.

51　Report by Mary Mohrer to Window Shop Board, April 4, 1970.

52　Letter from Mary Mohrer to executive committee in 1970. The day and date are unrecorded.

53　Executive committee report, January 7, 1971. French yo-yos were miniature toys that Mary Mohrer found at a trade show and displayed as novelties at the entrance of the Gift Shop.

54　Report by Cornelia McPeek, undated, but presumed to be late 1970.

55　Ibid.

56　Report by Cornelia McPeek, managing director, May 5, 1971.

57　President's Report, May 5, 1971.

58　Ibid.

59　Letter from Richard Kahan to employees, December 30, 1972.

60　Letter to Window Shop Board, December 25, 1972.

61　Interview with Dorothy Dahl, October 23, 2004.

62　Talk by Alice DeNormandie Cope at the Schlesinger Library, October 31, 1984.

63　Talk by Alice DeNormandie Cope at the Cambridge Historical Society, Nov. 17, 1974.

64　Lillian (Mrs. Robert) Alberty, Lore (Mrs. Konrad) Bloch, Grace (Mrs. Lee) Hasenbush, Priscilla (Mrs. Harold) Howe II, Anne (Mrs. William) King, Magda (Mrs. Laszlo) Tisza, Jeanne (Mrs. Frank) Westheimer, and Anne (Mrs. David Gordon) Wilson.

65　Interview of Dorothy Dahl, October 23, 2004.

66　Talk by Alice DeNormandie Cope at the Cambridge Historical Society, Nov. 17, 1974.

67 Interview with Mary Mohrer, October 16, 1984. Window Shop archives, Schlesinger Library.

68 Paper read by Marion Muller at the Mother's Study Club, Cambridge, April 1959.

69 "Curtain Falls for Window Shop," by Ellen Goodman, the *Boston Globe*, December 27, 1972, 31.

70 Board meeting, March 21, 1961.

71 Information on Mr. Bieringer is from the Summer Newsletter, 1985, of Facing History and Ourselves, 6–7. Other quotations and remembrances are from interviews with Dorothy Dahl in the 1980s.

72 Mary Johnson interview with Walter Bieringer, November 1, 1985. Window Shop archives, Schlesinger Library, box 1, folder 20.

73 See Chapter 2.

74 Letter, dated January 28, 1970.

75 "To the Rescue of the Learned: The Asylum Fellowship Plan at Harvard, 1938–40," *Harvard Library Bulletin*, Summer 1984, 205–38.

76 Cambridge: Harvard University Press, 1960.

77 Smithsonian Institution, 1965.

78 Boston: Little, Brown, 1975.

79 Letter from Margaret Earhart Smith to Elsa Ulich (Board President), June 12, 1942.

80 The *Radcliffe Quarterly*, November 1960.

81 Biographical information was taken from an unpublished work by Magdalena Padberg, "Das Leben der Elsa Brändström," and a brief biography by Elsa Bjorkman-Goldschmidt. Both works were translated into English by Charlotte H. Blaschke.

About the Authors

Ellen J. Miller was, for twenty-seven years, an administrator at Harvard Law School. She is co-editor of *All This Reading: The Literary World of Barbara Pym* (Fairleigh Dickinson University Press, 2003) and principal writer of *Images of America: Carlisle* (Arcadia Publishing Company, 2005). Her cousin was a long-time Window Shop employee.

Ilse Heyman is a Holocaust survivor who was assistant manager of the Window Shop Gift and Dress Shop for twenty-five years. In November 2005, she received a Peace and Justice Award from the City of Cambridge and is currently a member of the Peace Commission.

Dorothy Dahl joined the Window Shop Board in 1955 and served two terms as its president. After the shop closed, she presided over the Scholarship Fund until 1987. She is a board member of the Cambridge Center for Adult Education, which now occupies the Window Shop's former home.

Index

Alcalay, Albert, 40
Alexander, Fred, 52, *132*, 132–133, 163
Alexander, Jack, 132, 163
Alexander, Robert, 11, 132, 163
Aub, Elizabeth, xviii, 45, 55, *63*, 65–66, 69–70, 76, 131, *134*, 134–136, 158, 161, 163

Beauvais, Henry, 84, 163
Becher, Hertha, 10, 116, 132–133, 163
Bell, Lucille, 47, 51, 163
Benfey, Lotte, 3, 7, 25, 36, 38, 76, 78, *97*, 98–99, 116, 127, 163
Berger, Robert L., 56–57, 163
Bever, Marion, 7, 11, 28, 29, 56, 66, 82–83, 84, 90, 137–138, 146, 163, 172n19
Bibring, Grete, 2, 43
Bieringer, Walter, 37, 76–77, 131, 139–141, 163
Blumgart, Margaret S., 22, *130*, 172n17
Boehm, Alice, 17, 43, *100*, 100–103, 163
Brager, Adele, 20, 149
Brändström, Elsa. *see* Ulich, Elsa Brändström
Brandt, Chris, 101
Bridgman, Percy, 3
Bridgman, Percy, Mrs., 27
Broch, Alice (Perutz), xvii, 8, 19, 24–25, 26–28, 30, 32, 35, 36, 70, 71, *73*, 75–76, 80, 85, 98, *104*, 104–110, 116, 117, 125, *134*, 136, 137, 146, 163

Buka, Robert, 64
Bussgang, Julian, 55, 163

Cannon, Bernice, 63, 64, 146
Carpenter, Mrs., 12
Cohan, Lillian (Levin), 45, 90, 128, 164
Conant, James Bryant, 2–3
Cope, Alice DeNormandie, xvii, 3, 6–7, 14, 22, 25, 26, 28, 33, 34, 35, 36, 37, 54, 55, 58–59, 60, 62, 74, 77, 88, 93, 96, 105, 106, 109, 112–113, *130*, 131, 134–135, *142*, 142–145, 152, 155, 156, 163, 172n17, 172n19
Cope, Oliver, 113, 122, 131, 142
Cox, Constance, 93

Dahl, Dorothy, xiv–xv, xviii, 20, 45, 47, 61, 67, 87, 92, 94, 96, 107, 110, 138, 145, *146*, 146–147, 156, 158, 163
DeNormandie, Alice. *see* Cope, Alice
Dershowitz, Alan, 3
Deutsch, Helene, 2, 17, 72
Dunbar, Charles F., 22, *130*, 131, 172n17

Ehrlich, William, 22, 131, 172n17
Eisemann, Helen M., 22, *130*, 172n17
Eisenberg, Lotte, 76–77, 146, 164
Epstein, Herta, 16, 18, 19, 42

Fainsod, Johnnie, 172n19
Ferry, John, 131

978-0-595-40620-3
0-595-40620-3